The Brighton Ripper

David Arran

Published by New Generation Publishing in 2023

Copyright © David Arran 2023

First Edition

The author asserts the moral right under the Copyright, Designs and Patents Act 1988 to be identified as the author of this work.

All Rights reserved. No part of this publication may be reproduced, stored in a retrieval system or transmitted, in any form or by any means without the prior consent of the author, nor be otherwise circulated in any form of binding or cover other than that which it is published and without a similar condition being imposed on the subsequent purchaser.

ISBN
    Paperback   978-1-83563-065-5
    eBook   978-1-83563-066-2

www.newgeneration-publishing.com

New Generation Publishing

PROLOGUE

BECOMING JACK

In the glimmering half-light provided by a well-burned candle, the dark sinister figure of a tall, young man could be just about made out. He was standing and leaning over a large, aged, wooden table. A table that looked quite out of place, situated as it was, in the middle of the lounge of the period row house.

Lying on the table was the prostrated body of a woman. As the candle flickered, the dim grey light from it caught her motionless frame and the actual hideous events which were taking place, came into full view.

The young man stood over her was muttering madly under his breath. He was concentrating and busy, working in his action of sewing the woman's flesh with a long but quite substantial silver needle, and some very coarse-looking thread.

His nattering continued: They – that is those all around me – say I am quite mad, constantly talking to myself. But I know it is not just me that can hear my endless chattering. For, with some sort of a sixth sense, I know you are both nearby and listening.

And I'm right, aren't I?

Yes, you hang on to my every word and are wondering if it is you, personally, that I am talking to.

Well, I am!

So be sure to listen up. And listen up well. I promise you will be enthralled!

You do indeed catch me at such a very inopportune moment. Yes, here as I talk to you. I find my slightly panic-stricken self, stitching together the body of my latest murder victim.

Shocked are you? ………..Well, you shouldn't be!

This dreadful woman brought this fate upon herself and by her very own actions no less.

Who is she you ask?

Oh, Annie Smith, just another worthless shilling whore. A woman of no concern to you or indeed anyone at all. Even still, I am under so much pressure, for I have only the light of this slowly fading candle to see by and it is now almost half-burned down, so I have to work quickly.

Please then, I would ask you to forgive me of my curt chatter. I need to get her savaged torso sewn back together and buried soon. If not, I fear my latest deed of murder may be discovered and I may be caught and would surely be hung. I must admit, that I wish perhaps now I had not disembowelled the despicable woman so totally. But, when the madness that drives me to kill overcomes me, it is quite uncontrollable.

Anyway, I have replaced the woman's kidneys, pancreas and all of her intestines, as well as part of her uterus. Of course they now all remain completely detached from her internally. Oh, and I have left her liver, albeit a little diseased from excessive alcohol consumption, saved to one side of my table. Just here in fact, well one has to eat and when trimmed and fried it will be very welcome. Yes, welcome as a meal for me indeed. Times in these dreadful days of 1849 are hard and to eat every day is not a given, even for a young man such as I.

And who am I then? I now hear you ask. Oh yes, oh dear, how rude of me! Here am I mumbling on. Well, who am I?

Hah!

Now, that is the question.

One day I tell you this. Many folk would almost die to know, including I may add the local constables of this parish. But for now, you may call me.

Jack….. Jack…. Yes, that's me. It is true, I am just another, as you might say, face in the crowd at present. But in my conversation, do not lose your interest in me. Even as a young man, I still have a story to tell. And one, I promise you, that will keep you, from ever an easy sleep!

*****

Very well, if I have your ears, then I will begin:

Please excuse me whilst I pursue my stitching, but this latest corpse laid bare on my table must be concealed in earth and soonest, as I mentioned before.

Now where was I?

*****

Life for me began with privileges. I was born into a wealthy family in London's metropolis in the year 1829. However, even back in those early days as I was growing up, I somehow knew I was different.

My social skills were few and my need for order and a constant repetition of daily routine were obvious to all in my household. This, as I matured, was coupled with the compelling endless voices in my head, taunting me. Just as they do as I am here talking to you now. And these voices caused me such an irrationality of thoughts, that it was I suppose no wonder I would become a disturbed individual and live out a dysfunctional existence.

What an irony!

It makes me laugh to think of it, me mentioning my ill mental health as I tell you of my past, standing over a blood-soaked body killed by my own hand. Hardly the deed of a sane man perhaps you may think? But I have my reasons which will become clear; that I promise you!

For all my early issues, shall we say? I was gifted as a scholar and had a fascination for English both in language and written literature. My particular skill, my tutors quickly recognised, was in poetry.

Indeed, my love of rhyme and poetic prose I used as an outlet in my formative years. Mostly to convey the mixed emotions and feelings I had running constantly in my mind and indeed to hide those thoughts, that to survive without ridicule, I kept inside and totally within myself.

*****

There we are! A little chaotic but that is this wretched woman's midriff nearly sewn. Not neat I confess, as I am rushed, but at least nearly completed.

I digress.

So sorry, but I do find my mind does flit so. I find it hard to concentrate at times, but yes, I will continue...

Well, it was by the hand of fate that I was also blessed, along with a gift for learning, by being tall and fair of face. One might even say handsome.

On this point, I would add that it is amazing how accepting people can be of you, no matter how much they consider you to be odd or different if you are blessed with money and good looks. Such hypocrisy I suppose is found in all of us, even me to a greater or lesser extent.

*****

So, London was the city I grew up in and it was an overcrowded and depressing place overall. Although, of course, I was lucky in that my family was wealthy. But I still knew one did not have to venture far, even from my large home, to find many people desperate and struggling just to survive.

After the completion of my education, I managed to secure a place as a student doctor at the prestigious Royal London Hospital in Whitechapel and my early studies went very well. My still slightly odd behaviour was now kindly referenced as eccentric, and I could enjoy killing and dissecting a whole variety of poor defenceless animals without anyone turning a hair, all of course in the name of scientific learning!

I was even allowed to dissect some human corpses. These cadavers were most welcomed by me, and I did enthuse in their study and disembowelling, with great ardour. The knowledge I gained in fact from such cadavers does assist me now. In this the task I undertake here before you, working on this freshly slaughtered carcass.

Anyhow, back to my tale.

*****

Time went on and one cold dark winter's evening I found myself approached by an attractive young woman, as I walked the busy streets on the way to my lodgings. In truth, I would normally take a carriage at the end of my day, but sometimes I chose to walk the streets on my way home, as if with some strange urge to watch all the life taking place around me. I also had a strange compunction to learn and find my way around the many passageways of Whitechapel, although at the time of course I knew not why the layout of such a vile place enthralled me so.

Well as I walked I was accosted by this young woman as I said. And at first, I gave her scant regard. For many a time, a prostitute did approach me to try and secure my physical interest in her body and earn perhaps a shilling or more by so doing. My appearance you see, gave away my being a young man of some means. As such, I knew I ran the risk of being robbed especially in these shall we say less desirable city streets. Anyway, finally, this woman cornered me in one of the small alleyways and begged me for my help.

"Please, sir, stop and wait up. I need your help. Please, please wait. I just need one minute of your time kind sir. I need your advice as a doctor," she pleaded.

She had seen me before or knew of me in some way. Because it was my professional help that I now learned from her bleating, that she sought. Considering my conscience I stopped and the young woman's ordeal was revealed.

It became apparent to me that she was a prostitute, called Catherine Thompson and she found herself in some dilemma. She had discovered she was with child. A child she neither wanted nor indeed had the means to support.

"I am desperate, sir," she wept. "I beg of you to just examine me if only to allay my fears or confirm them," she cried.

After a quick deliberation and now in my taking some pity on her desperation, I finally agreed to return to the young woman's dwelling place with her. A foul and unpleasant dark, damp, single room awaited us both and this was where I was to examine her.

The young woman was, as she had feared, with child. She continued with her begging for me to help her end this unwanted pregnancy.

"You must help me, sir. I have barely the means to support myself. I do not ask you to perform such a deed just for me. It is the best choice for all concerned. Only the workhouse awaits me and the child, and that as you know for yourself is no life. Help me. I beg you, sir."

I knew sadly she was right and that if I ignored her wishes I was surely condemning her and the child to an intolerable existence. However, I knew also I must be mindful of the harshness of the penalties I would be risking and the laws I would be breaking in performing such an operation, so at first I resisted her requests with much adamance.

This young woman, however, was not for giving up and she did go on so and with much persistence. I found my opposition weakening and my interest being stimulated by the thought of actually being able to operate on a living person. So, despite my complete lack of any previous experience, I finally relented and agreed to help her.

"God bless you, kind sir," she said, now weeping with joy. "It must be soon. For I cannot delay another day, I beg you, sir. Can I say in the morning, just after ten tomorrow?"

The time was arranged and I turned up at the young woman's residence with just my very limited surgical instruments and a wire brush, that I had read could be used as an implement to cause the abortion I had conceded to undertake. There was little hygiene in such an abode and my instruments were far from correctly sterile, but she as the patient was insistent I go ahead and so I began.

It was then that a strange feeling swept over me. The young woman had no sedation and as I worked she started to bleed profusely and was crying out loudly with pain. Something in me was awakened, something evil, all- consuming. I suddenly found myself muffling her voice by placing my large hand over her mouth whilst repeatedly and more violently forcing my instrument of abortion into her. I couldn't stop myself.

The blood and her cries of agony excited me, terrified me and drove me to attack her further. I don't know how long it all lasted, but finally, she passed out and the whole of her bedding was soaked with her deep red blood. With a sudden sense of derealisation, I was myself once again and back in the room. The passing of what I can only describe as an awful madness was gone from my being. I now grabbed at her bed sheet and wiped frantically at the sanguine fluid covering the apron I had put on to undertake my awful operation. It was hopeless as there was simply far too much blood. So I ripped it from me, grabbed my few surgical items and fled from the place, leaving the woman with the wire brush I had forced into her, still embedded in her now heavily blooded vagina.

Into the street, I ran from her dwelling. Covered in the young woman's blood, I was confused, panicked and frightened. Some people called after me as I ran, but I knew I dared not stop. Others, thinking I had been the victim of an attempted robbery, tried to chase me and see what events had occurred to get me in such a bloody and skittish state.

My knowledge of the Whitechapel passageways now

aided me greatly in my escape. Finally, I managed to wave down a carriage, jump into it and I hurriedly told the driver to just go. He too thought I must have been attacked and urged his horse on its way with some haste.

After giving him my directions, the carriage dropped me off near to my lodgings. I paid the driver, reassured him I would be okay and went inside the residence, shutting the door to my room hard behind me and thankful to have not been seen to enter the house by anyone else.

When I looked through the front bay window of my room, the coach was gone. I was home and safe, just shaken. I knew full well, that the young woman on whom I had just operated could never have survived the ordeal and this fact was confirmed the next morning by my landlady.

This was a busy body old woman; an old woman who took great interest in any local gossip. She could not wait to tell me, how a young prostitute in Whitechapel had been found dead when she brought me my morning tea. She said a local constable had described the killing, as a particularly brutal and failed attempt at an illegal abortion. Delighting in telling me every fact of the matter she knew, as well as others she invented and chose to exaggerate.

*****

Back to my latest corpse, here on this table – her midriff is now completely sewn together. Good we are pleased are we not? So let us look at stitching the woman's cut-throat. It is one part of her mangled frame that I have still to sew. Look! It is severed from under her right ear to almost underneath the lowest part of her left ear. The skin covering the shattered cartilage of the throat is paper thin and is extremely difficult to stitch with any precision. In addition, this kitchen table is not exactly ideal to work on. But we will persevere, won't we?

Anyway, this stiffening corpse aside, I will, as I am sure you had hoped to hear, continue with my tale.

*****

Well, following those awful events I did not venture from my lodging house for the next two whole days. I had burned all my blood-stained clothing, setting it alight on the fire in the grate of my lounge, to be rid of it and to hide any link to myself and my crime.

Perplexed still, I was so very unsure of what exactly I should do next. My rapidly increasing anxiety caused me such dreadful thoughts in my mind, such thoughts to nearly drive me insane with fear. Finally, I decided I would be missed in my studies at the hospital. I made up my mind to attend and perhaps confide in my mentor Professor Worthington. I was desperate by this time to share the overwhelming burden of my worry.

After what seemed an eternal age in the hospital and long after my first few study classes were completed, I managed to approach the professor alone in his study. It was no surprise I suppose, that following such a stressful time holding all I had undergone over the past few days to myself, my composure was lost. I blurted out my story of how I had tried to help this young woman in her predicament of pregnancy and the resulting occurrence of her death.

I must admit to you, too, as my only true confidant, that I did not reveal to the professor the madness that had overcome me leading to those terrible events. I suppose in the fear, he would think me insane, just like all the others in my life.

The professor, had by some chance, read about the incident in the paper. He was visibly shocked by my confession. He asked me who else I had told of these events and seemed at least relieved when I told him, it was only his good self I had confided in. My mind was not my own again by this time, for I was in total panic as he talked about police and law and so many other potential consequences for my actions. Then his tone changed. As if in a sudden realisation, a realisation of what damming repercussions this scandal could bring on the hospital and perhaps his position as such a hospital senior.

He told me straight away to go. That I must leave the hospital immediately, that I would be discharged and that this was now the only course of action open to him. He added I would receive a letter from him regarding his decision the next morning.

"Yes, leave," he said. "Just go. And this must never, never be mentioned again."

I pleaded with him for some alternative solution, but it was hopeless. He told me quite sternly that I would not be reported to the police for the illegal abortion I had been party to. But only if I left the hospital there and then and never went back.

*****

Even as I stitch this woman's throat, those events still disturb me and fill me with dread. My career was gone. I was desperate and alone. Worse still I knew I could confide in no one. My already fragile mental state was near breaking point and there was more heartache yet to come for me.

After leaving the hospital I returned to my lodging to collect all my things and immediately took a carriage to my family home. My welcome here too was not as I had hoped. My own family, as I have mentioned previously, had always regarded me as odd and different. My father and mother had found my conduct far too challenging and had chosen to move away when I was just a young boy. I had, as a result of this, been taken in and given a good home by my rich uncle, who thought, in turn, he could cure my difference of behaviour, by regular brutal beatings.

Only my securing a place as a student doctor in such a well-respected hospital as London's very own Royal had earned me a little acclaim from them all. Now to just turn up on my uncle again, out of the blue so to speak and tell him of my discharge from this respectable position, without any plausible explanation was more than he could bear. I knew, however, that whatever else I did, I dared not tell him exactly why I had been discharged. Therefore it was inevitable I suppose that I would now be disowned next by him as well.

"We find you back here, young man. I thought finally you had changed for the better. Well, we have tried, but your aunt and I must now wash our hands of you. You had your chance of a good career and have thrown it away. Best we think you leave and do not come back," he said.

Thus it was. I received a sum of money from my own family, just to leave and never return. My uncle said when I had secured a place to live, money would be sent to me if I forwarded him my address. Sent on only, to keep me from returning home ever again and if ever I did so, he threatened I would lose all my income and would surely become destitute.

This second turning out from my own family, coupled with all the recent stress over the events that had taken place, was the final straw for me mentally. I was broken. It was after this rejection, that I sought solace in talking to the one person I could always rely on.

Myself.

I started to chatter continuously to myself under my breath. Only convincing everyone I met even more of my total madness. But at least now I have you to chatter to and you always listen. I am sure you are there and I take some comfort in your interest in me. Even if it is only your macabre desire to discover what will become of me.

*****

I moved to Brighton, London by the sea and easy to travel to. But still a place where nobody knew me, or from where I came. The streets of Brighton too were crowded, a mirror image virtually in fact of the London I had left behind. My only blessing was that I had some money, an income, even if it was only secured by staying away from my family and the hiding of my past life. This at least meant I would not become one of the many poor souls, who just literally begged an existence.

I took a room at an inn, the Cricketers in Black Lion Street, adjacent to the Brighton Lanes. This old public house would be my new home for my first few nights here. I had made up my mind to try to normalise my life. I would fight the demons in my head. Yes, I still talked to myself, which everyone I met found slightly odd. But this was Brighton and its acceptance of all and any persons, even those out of the society norm, was apparent even then. I drank in the bar and soon found several new friends, who encouraged me of course to repeatedly buy them all drinks.

In some sort of irony, my closest new friend was a local ageing prostitute. A woman called Annie Smith. The woman lying here prostrated on this very table, dead. She latched onto me, almost from the minute I stepped into the crowded bar and seemed genuinely interested in me as a person. She didn't seem to care that I was shy and withdrawn and was happy to fight my corner for me, even when some others in the bar raised the issue of me talking to myself.

"Leave him alone," she said. "He is a gentleman, not like you common sods. I like the way he talks," she added. "He treats a lady, like a lady."

"Do you know any ladies then, Annie?" another man at the bar said. All around him, there was a ripple of raucous laughter.

"Ignore them, handsome," she said.

The woman took my hand and led me to the other end of the bar where it was quieter. In some strange way, I thought I could trust her. She was the first person who for a long time had seemed to show me any kindness. She was very clever at winning a man's trust I later discovered. Especially a man with a fat purse, but I was ignorant of these facts at this time.

"This public house is not at all a place you should be staying," she said. "Buy me another gin and when the night ends come back to my place. I share with three other girls, but we have a room spare which would be quiet and the rent would be far less than here. This is not the place for a man such as you, Jack," she added.

She was of course right. She could see, even though I tried desperately to hide it, that the constant loud noise of the bar unnerved me and the many brawls and lewd goings on I found difficult to deal with.

"Yes," she said. "You will not stay here a moment longer, Jack. You are coming home with me. Gather your things."

I moved into 19 Compton Street, the home of this woman, Annie Smith, who lived there along with three other prostitutes. At first, life was more bearable there for me. All the women were kind enough and I felt we were all able to coalesce. Yes, they were all common prostitutes, but they had an arrangement with their landlord. An arrangement which ensured they, shall we say, did not pay their rent with money but worked for it in his company a couple of times a week. Often he had three of them in one bed at a time and I had to go out whenever he came to the house and walk the streets for a few hours, as the noise of their disgusting behaviour troubled me so.

The women had cleared the largest bedroom out for me to occupy and I in turn paid them my rent, in cash, in advance. They also encouraged me to go to the Cricketers and several other public houses in their company most evenings. Where I would in my naivety, buy all the drinks consumed. Usually, until the women were all either quite drunk or had disappeared, with a man friend or two.

Annie made a pass at me, in a sexual fashion, quite early on in my stay at the property. But I never had any inclination for such things and told her so quite adamantly. Indeed, my lack of sexual interest in women helped them feel more at ease with me in their home and I genuinely hoped they just liked me as a person. Until:

*****

Well, one evening just before we were all due to go out as usual to the Cricketers, I happened to go downstairs. When I reached the bottom of the stairs I could hear the four women laughing and chatting quite loudly. I was mumbling to myself, as is my way, but quietly and they did not hear me nor sense my approach. As I went to go into the lounge I happened to hear my name mentioned. Anyway curiosity got the better of me, and foolishly I stood just by the slightly opened door and listened.

"That Jack, what an odd fellow he is," one of the prostitutes said.

"Well he pays us good rent," I heard Annie reply.

"Yes, Annie, but you told us yourself before bringing him here, that he was not all there, didn't you? And you said he has a fat purse we can empty and we do that nearly every evening."

The women all chuckled.

"And how does he get that money I wonder? I suspect he has a rich family who pay him to stay away," one said.

The giggling women went on.

"He has no interest in us either," another said.

"Have you ever known a man like that? Most just can't wait to get into your knickers."

"He is just not normal," another replied.

The four women laughed. All had been drinking and

had no clue I was standing at the door listening.

"And his constant muttering, he is mad, quite mad I think," one of the women said. "He should be in an institution perhaps?"

"You saw him too, didn't you, Annie? Tell the girls what you told me when you spied on him taking a bath."

The four laughed again.

"No I shouldn't," Annie replied. "He is a harmless lost soul and we like his money. When it runs out, though, we will be best rid of him, girls," she went on. "But yes, I did see him and he has the tiniest manhood I have ever been witness to. Nothing to bother us or any other woman ever there," she said and laughed loudly along with the other three women.

I stood at the door devastated, these four women that I thought liked me, respected me and understood me, were little more than liars and cheats. Tearful and shaking, I felt like such a fool and a failure. I had been taken advantage of, once again, by women who were nothing more than common whores.

A whore had cost me my whole life in London and now this group was going to try and destroy me again. Something inside me snapped then and there. My mind was overtaken by the devil and thoughts of retribution. There was no turning back to sanity now. Things were going to be different and I swore, muttering faster to myself, that vengeance would be mine.

I walked away from the door and crept back up the stairs. The time was not right, despite the anger and hurt that welled up inside me, to attack all four women. No, I must be clever, and patient to plan their individual demise. For yes killing them was what I had decided to do, and in my new state of complete madness, I wanted them all to suffer unimaginably before they died, each last worthless whore one of them.

That evening we ventured out as usual. But all four women commented on how muted my mood seemed and with such hypocrisy, they asked if I was feeling quite well. Soon though they were all drunk and flirting with any number of men, whose favour they thought they might win over and sell their slut bodies to. How I now despised them all; in fact, I despised the whole dreadful place. The stench of the alcohol and the rawness of such common people disturbed me more than ever. I made some excuse to Annie, who barely noticed my leaving and I walked home slowly in the light rain, plotting my revenge.

Two days later I had moved.

Oh, they all resisted my leaving initially, but not because they would miss me, no all they would miss was my purse. Fortuitously, I discovered a property to rent in the very same street as the whores, in fact just a few doors down from them. My new home was to be number 13 Compton Street. I sighted some continuance of several made-up symptoms of ill health, as my reason for moving out so suddenly. Of course, in truth, I had no such symptoms. But with the recent deadly outbreaks in the town of Cholera, none of the women made major objections to my leaving.

Recently at 13 Compton Street, Cholera had wiped out a family of eight and because of this there was little interest to occupy it, despite so many people being homeless or struggling to find somewhere to reside. The populous also were ignorant of the disease, and the way it was contracted. I, with my medical training, knew it was spread usually through contaminated water and that if I cleaned through the dwelling properly I should be safe from the dreadful illness.

Given these facts, I offered the landlord a rent that was affordable to me and he readily accepted with no hesitation. Now I had a base, some peace to settle myself and I had time. All the time I needed to plot my murderous revenge.

"Get yourself well and come back to us," the deceitful whore Annie had said to me as I left. "We will miss you here," she added.

No longer however could they use me and take me for a fool; now would be the time I would make them pay for all their dreadful deceit.

Ironically my mood had changed. This sudden shock and upset had not only made me despise the whores, but it also had in some way given me confidence. A strange feeling of inner strength and purpose was surging through my being. Although I still constantly chattered to myself, I felt more able to communicate with others. I no longer felt subservient to anyone; I found an arrogance perhaps it was just anger, but something in me was changing. I was evolving, even unbeknown to me at this time, into the killer who one day would shock the whole world. My destiny awaited me, but for now, I would plot day and night, on just how I could slaughter and inflict unimaginable suffering on those four spiteful bitches.

Over the next few days, I watched the whores as they came and went from the house. I soon had worked out their routines. They all had a regular clientele who they visited or places they frequently went, to meet men who they could pick up and would have use of their personal services.

I had decided my medical training would not be

wasted. I knew human anatomy well and how to inflict the most brutal and devastating wounds. My surgical instruments would no longer be left idle in an unused Gladstone bag and as I polished them one by one, whilst sitting in the lounge at my new home, a self-satisfying evil grin painted across my face. I would throttle the women, after hunting them individually and then as they were just about conscious and could feel every wound, I would rip them open like a sack of grain. The conclusion of which would see them beg me for death, as a release from their suffering. My plan was hatched, my evil self was awakened and I was ready… to kill.

*****

The first of my victims was chosen. Sarah. She was the youngest and the prettiest. She also had tormented me the most and had been the least understanding of my 'tics', when I had initially moved into their home. It felt somehow, only right that she should be the first to die because of this, *I do so hope you agree*. Yes of course you do. We know don't we, her penance awaited her and it filled me with such a sense of purpose and well-being. To know finally, for every ill-fated hand I had been dealt in life, that someone would pay and how they would pay, with their very own lives.

I had followed the young prostitute, unbeknownst to her of course, for the past couple of weeks and had discovered that she often walked home past the coach house stables courtyard in the early hours of a Tuesday morning, after visiting the home of a regular client.

The horses in the stables were often noisy and I realised that this building would be the perfect place to slaughter the young whore as any strange sounds emulating from there would be ignored by passers-by. Everything was in place and I felt a real sense of nervous excitement as I donned my frock coat and my top hat.

I picked up my Gladstone bag and having done so put a fresh white handkerchief in my coat pocket. I knew if the woman screamed, I could perhaps ball this up and force it into her mouth to keep her quiet whilst I throttled her. I also placed into my other coat pocket a larger black cloth, which I intended to wear to partially cover my face when I attacked her, so she would not initially recognise me.

One quick admiring glance in the long mirror of my bedroom and looking just like a doctor on call, I stepped out into the cold early hours of the morning, still mumbling to myself words of continuing encouragement. "It is time, Jack, it is time. Those whores must pay for what they have done. They must pay, they must!"

The first whore's death was followed shortly after by the second and then the third and so on over several weeks. Each killing was more savage than the last. By the time I slaughtered this last wretched shilling whore Annie Smith, the woman lain here before me. I was not only disembowelling my victims totally but was also removing their organs, their tongues and even their eyelids, to satisfy my worsening madness.

Oh yes, I do realise I am quite mad but prefer to think I have been driven so by circumstance and thereby find myself the way with it all, to sleep without the guilt of conscience almost every night.

I have been questioned twice and released for these murders by the local parish constabulary, but with a few well-placed shillings in the right palm's I have bought a provided alibi. Alibi's which have seen me in the company of either a man or indeed a loose woman of no morality, at the time of every killing. Alibi's as watertight as the bladder used to hold the water I now drink from. If only the constables could see me now!

*****

There I am finished with this corpse, she is sewn together. Done to keep the body in a whole state and make it easier to bury. Though I must admit the woman has lost her looks in death and is no longer a pretty sight, even to my eye. The hole is dug, previously I might add, with much toil on my part and I am ready now to carry the corpse to it and complete my wicked deed. I will continue with my tale, though, for I can shovel and speak at one time.

Goodness! She is heavier than I first thought! It is a piece of good fortune for me that this small garden is not directly overlooked and in such blackness of the night, the candle I carry, lights only the excavated earth, just enough for me to see and place the body into. Her clothing and attire now must follow, and then I can complete the burial.

My candle is now all but burned out, but I am done. Annie Smith, the common prostitute, no longer exists in this world. For myself and my evading of capture, I must admit I sincerely hope that she remains hidden in this earth forever. Now I must cover this grave with these old sacks and let nature take its course, to overgrow this burial pit with vegetation.

*****

Oh curse! What a time to have the door knocked! I will do my best to ignore it, for I certainly cannot have any caller here whilst I am in this predicament. The body yes, lies in the ground and hidden, but I am awash with blood and soil.

Bother, the door knocks again and louder this time. I have no choice but to see who is calling. I will shut and lock the door to the back garden and hasten to see who bangs my front door so repeatedly.

"Open up it is the police. Open this door or we will break it down."

The constabulary, oh no and so I am done for. I opened the door and then I was pushed to the floor by three large constables.

"Who are you talking to?" one of the constables asks me.

I do not tell him but instead continue in my muttering to you, which they just attribute to my madness. The wretched whore's liver is found on my table by a constable, which is still freshly covered with blood, as am I.

Within the next hour, I am locked in a police cell and am visited by many officers, who peer through the small inspection hatch, keen to see for themselves the man capable of such a string of barbaric murders.

My muttering also strangely fascinates them. Though I fear the process of law will not be long in producing me before a judge and jury, to which my obvious insanity will afford me no defence.

Despite their constant questioning of me, I refuse to reveal where the remains of Annie Smith are hidden. In their ignorance, they cannot it seems, detect she is buried in the garden of my very own dwelling. They seem so preoccupied with congratulating themselves on my capture, that they miss this, the most obvious scenario.

I must admit to be apprehended by such incompetent fools is totally shameful on my part. But at least I can rest in my cell, knowing every last one of those vile whores lies slaughtered by my own hand.

*****

It is done and the self-righteous judge in all his pompous splendour dons the black cap and I am surely sentenced to hang by the neck until I am dead. His honour, what hypocrisy, for I have seen this man in the company of many of the whores who I have slain. The judge orders my name to be struck from all records, so I shall receive no notoriety or a place in written history for my heinous crimes. Thus my anonymity is secured in this life.

The next two days that I pass in my small barren cell seem to last forever. Though I just wish to be left unattended with my thoughts I am visited endlessly by any number of priests seeking to save my soul and a multitude of reporters anxious, to sell for me, my story. What little regard I now hold for either.

Finally, in due course, I hear the rattle of keys ringing from the belt of the jailer, who is to escort me to my place of execution. His being is quiet and I fear he would jump for his life, were I to say '*BOO*' to him, but I resist the temptation. My scaring days on this earth as a mortal soul, are well done.

The executioner places a hood upon my head and with my hands bound, I see only the darkness of Hell that awaits me. I do not hear the mechanism of the trap door opening but feel myself falling endlessly into blackness.

The rope marks my broken neck well, and thus it is the end of my mortal life. But with the end of any person, there is the chance of a life to follow.

Did you not know?

Oh yes, it is true and never doubt it!

For the choices are yours to be made in a good life or a wicked one. My choices of course were already made for me, simply because my mortal soul was so evil.

Thus I was taken into the care of the masters of the dark matter, those who rule Hell unseen and who seek to upset the Gods of goodness with deeds of malice, evil and wickedness. And as such keep as many persons as possible from the gates of Heaven.

Recruited you might say I was. Yes, recruited, I like that, and I will when my masters decree it so, return to be murderous once again on your Earth. Very soon will I, now immortal, step through the very fabric of time itself.

In addition, and as a reward for my evil doings in my earthly existence, my masters have gifted me the soul of my last victim, Annie Smith, the whore most despised by me. In this servitude, she is cursed to travel with me for all time. Her duty will be to prepare my way for my comings back to your Earth. There will be much work for her to do if I am to slip into all and any society unnoticed.

Her earthly form will be, an aged old woman. Chosen by me to be haggard and suffering, quite aptly for this wretched female I feel.

And mine?

Well quite rightly as her master, a gentleman. Yes,

the irony of it suits me. A Victorian gentleman no less!

After all a top hat befits me, as indeed does some smart attire.

Although my appearance I may choose to change as required. Oh and a Gladstone bag. Yes, I could almost be a doctor! And of course, I must carry my surgical instruments to commit my murderous undertakings. My method of murder will not change over time. I do feel ripped and disembowelled corpses hold a certain terror of their own to humanity. And terror after all is my business.

Oh and one more thing. Yes, I may travel through time immortal for sure. But my evil masters, in their pursuit of this terror, have inflicted on me one more curse.

If ever I am captured I will become mortal again and on my demise my soul will cease to exist, and for all of time. Thus the stakes of my adventures could not be higher, for either me or my victims. This game of life and death is to be played out and played out by the rules of the devils of Hell themselves until I am captured.

Now, for the first time, I stumble through the stygian darkness that is Hell. The clock etched on the hands of time, not having to move too far forward. The masters of the dark matter have gifted me an early return to Earth, to enjoy the murders so horrific they wish me to undertake.

*****

A strange fog hangs eerie in the crowded dirty streets. The year is 1888 and in the darkest corner of an alleyway, I begin to appear. I draw in a huge breath of the damp, dank, air that gives my form life again and I set off walking.

I smile to myself, for this is a place I know well. Whitechapel, London and here I have arrived to make my name of infamy, killing whores.

For all the anonymity of my previous murders in history, these killings I now undertake will be the first ones in which I make my mark in the world. Where my murders will be so terrifying, the world will remember them for all eternity. And I will become known forever:

As: *Jack*

Jack The Ripper!

But enough of this…….*The whores are plentiful here… And I have murders to prepare for!*

*****

Thus the murders at Whitechapel made my name. The infamy of these killings is well written into the annals of history and I will not dwell on these. For you, the reader of this tale, know of these events already and surely have more interest in where I, 'Jack the Ripper', will appear next.

Read on and all will become clear:

But beware! My latest exploits are not for the faint-hearted.

Indeed, the more time I spend immortal and not apprehended, the more my blood lust and the demands from my evil masters from the dark matter increase.

You have been warned!

*****

Unencumbered by morals of soul,
I stalk the streets with just one goal,
And every victim I do fell,
Is just a whore of ne'er do well,
They cannot catch me, hear them cry,
Both law and vigilante try,
But know not who or what I be,
So I'll rip them all and still be free,
Synonymous with fear my name,
With Whitechapel my hall of fame,
But be you sure not just this place,
Will only see this killer's face,
In all and every history,
Look hard and "Jack" you'll always see,
The infamous travels of the tripper,
Time has labelled…"Jack the Ripper."

THE BRIGHTON RIPPER

CHAPTER ONE

Brighton and Hove is reputedly one of the most haunted cities in England. With its famous Brighton Lanes and Black Lion Street being home to what is believed to be the town's oldest public house, The Cricketers. According to legend, this established drinking place has long had a supposed close historical link to the now infamous tales of, *'Jack the Ripper'*. It is still said to this day, by some, to be where 'Jack' stayed and planned his murderous undertakings in Whitechapel. Indeed, the public house and the surrounding lanes have long been famous for many a ghostly apparition of the 'Ripper', who supposedly can appear and disappear, at will.

Our story begins in Brighton's city centre, on 9th November 1988, an especially damp, cold day. One hundred years, as a matter of fact, after the last reported killing of those historical London murders. This particular day in the city had been uneventful to this moment, but that was about to change.

It was late afternoon when the inky black outline of a tall figure seemed to just step out from one of the crumbling brick walls that, together, form the eerie mini maze, of the Brighton Lanes. These narrow lanes with their historic cobbled-style streets twist and turn in numerous directions throughout a small self-contained group of tunnel-like passageways, which are found situated in the very heart of the City of Brighton itself.

Supposedly haunted and roamed by a variety of ghoulish apparitions, in these more modern times they are punctuated with a miscellany of small shops and enterprising businesses. They still, however, in their unique cobbled passageway form, lend themselves to any insightful visitor, to an imagining that they are stepping backward through time. A place, perhaps, where one feels Victorian characters could actually come back to life and suddenly materialize around any corner, at any moment.

Just before this tenebrous figure appeared, a very unusual heavy fog had descended quite suddenly upon the city. The fog itself was it seemed, heaviest in its form around the lanes themselves and it enclosed them and crept along every one of the many mini passageways, with an unearthly ghostly stealth. The density of this fog was making the shape in the shadow hard to see clearly at first, as it loitered in the half-light, at a corner of one of the darkest passageways linking Black Lion Street and the lanes and within touching distance of 'The Cricketers' public house.

The figure moved forward slightly and stepped away from the semi-darkness of the wall. As it did so the all-consuming haze seemed to lift slowly, almost as if in a response to this movement. The remaining fog crept slowly upwards and started to dissipate and the tall silhouette of a man could just about be made out. The lanes themselves were quiet at this time of the year, and especially so in the late afternoon on such a damp, cold day. This particular passageway too, was deserted at this time, apart from this sole spooky male apparition.

The man ceased his forward motion and stood for a moment perfectly stationary. Then, as if slowly coming to life again, he lifted his head and drew a purposeful deep breath of the damp air that surrounded him. Such was this intake of breath that it lifted his whole diaphragm upward filling his lungs to their full capacity. It was a gasping for air; not unlike perhaps the first breath of a new life.

The stranger held onto this deep breath for just a short time and then exhaled. He took another breath, but this time as he released it he shook violently and with such intensity that his whole body frame could be seen to shudder. There was some sort of a visible reaction taking place within him. The shudder became more aggressive and his whole torso was now shaking, almost as if each section of his body was being afforded oxygen too fast. This contortion quickly passed, and the man started to visibly relax. His quivering frame was still once more and he stood quite fixed in his posture for a moment. He moved again, this time in a controlled and deliberate way, rolling his neck, stretching and elongating his ligaments in an exacting and methodical motion. He was concentrating on each movement, pausing in deliberation before making them.

After casting his eyes downwards he examined and stretched his arms and hands, pulling at each tendon and sinew testing them. He continued this sequential exploration of movement, systematically and individually proving the function of each of his fingers and clenching and unclenching each hand in turn. His facial expression changed, and he gave a cold almost self-gratifying smile.

With the dense and inexplicable blanket of fog having all but completely cleared, the man's actual physical appearance and clothing could be focused on.

It was obvious that he was wearing clothes from the Victorian era. He appeared extremely smart and tailored, with an immaculate dark dress coat, smart black trousers and highly polished black boots. Facially he had a ruddy soft complexion, with two thick bushy sideburns and a manicured thin moustache.

His posture was both upright and regimented. Slim and muscular he appeared to be aged about thirty. He had a dark presence about him that was almost tangible. On his head he wore a smart black, beautifully finished top hat. This shiny very ornate headwear made him look very tall and only added to his masculine physical bearing as he stood there, a lone ghostly figure in the gloomy shadows. His left hand grasped the handles of a pristine polished black, surgeon's style, Gladstone bag and this he gripped with such force, that it whitened his tensioned knuckles.

In any town other than Brighton, which is a city known for being a place where nothing is out of the norm, his attire would probably have shocked and startled a young gay couple who had by chance just come around the corner and into the narrow lanes. The two very relaxed young men walked past him holding hands and seemed to take his appearance in their stride.

"Nice outfit," the younger of the two men said and they both smiled mischievously while eyeing the man up. He gave no response but lifted his black piercing eyes until they met with theirs and then proceeded to give both men such a stare that it halted them in their tracks for a second. Although visibly shaken by the look they had been given, the pair then resumed their progress and carried on walking past the stranger.

One could be heard to say, "What a fucking freak!" To which his young friend replied, "And did you see his eyes!?"

The moment passed, their conversation changed and their speech could be heard to fade away into the darkness and distance, as they continued on their way.

Seemingly having gathered his bearings, the tall stranger walked slowly forward. His first couple of steps were laboured and sluggish. However, after a few more paces his singularity of movement became more synchronised and he, with increasing momentum, set off heading out of the Brighton Lanes.

The man reached the end of the Lanes and paused for a split second, checking himself briefly again with a downward glance of his midriff. He then proceeded to cross the small Ship Street road. Inadvertently he stepped straight out, not watching where he was going, and appearing oblivious to the continuous passing collection of urban Brighton traffic. Several cars stopped and tooted horns at him in their frustration at his standing in the carriageway.

Now leaving Ship Street, he turned left into the busier bustling North Street. His dark figure more awakened, he was striding purposefully up the road. He still seemed to ignore his surroundings, including the many people who gave him the occasional stare and the vast array of busy shops. The stranger appeared only as an automaton, driven and intensely focused as if programmed with instructions to reach some predetermined destination.

His journey continued and the prevailing dampness hung thickly in the air, as the late afternoon darkness was slowly drawing in. Rounding the corner, he left the bustle of the main city centre and turned into the much quieter Dyke Road where he saw the figure of an old woman walking slowly and purposefully toward him.

He seemed to focus on her. His manner changed slightly and his pace became slower. She appeared to have a strange magnetism he could not resist and he drifted in her direction, as if lured and totally captivated by her presence.

The old, dishevelled woman was of a frail frame. She was petite and her gait was marked by a cumbersome and obvious limp. This limp caused her left leg to drag slightly behind her and caused the heel of her left shoe to claw at the pavement. She wore a black, heavily knitted shawl and a long black dress with a pair of thick black tights. On her feet, she wore a pair of shiny black boots, with small well-worn heels. She had a slight stoop and was hunched over in her posture.

Barring these two oddest of figures, the street was empty at this time and as they passed one another both paused for a second, seemingly to recognise each other. The dishevelled old woman reached out and took hold of the dark, handsome man's hand and with her gnarled, scrawny fingers, pressed a shiny, single, silver key that she was holding, hard into his left palm. Without even lifting her eyes and in an almost throttled quivering voice she whispered. "Hello, Master Jack." She then paused for a brief moment and added. "All is prepared for your coming."

Looking down and now directly at her, the man replied quietly. "Together once again, so we are, Annie."

The old woman gave no response to this statement and then as if her duty here was completed, she shuffled on her way and she did not attempt to look back.

CHAPTER TWO

A group of young gay men laughed raucously as they sat around a candlelit table, in the front of a small cosy town centre bar. The bar was filled to bursting by an eclectic group of predominantly male customers, wearing everything from tight leather trousers to dresses. The young men at the table were chatting, sharing their day's events on that early evening and relaxing in what they held as almost a sanctum. Amongst them was a young Polish man, Jakub Kowalski, who was being enthusiastically quizzed, by two others at the table, on what life was like for a student doctor at the local hospital. "I am still finding it hard to adjust," the young man said. "I have been there such a short time and there is so much pressure on me at the moment."

He was not exaggerating. Kowalski had come to Britain to study medicine and had secured a place at the prestigious Royal London Hospital in Whitechapel. However, because of his underachieving performance and a lack of study ethic, he was sent to the Royal Sussex County Hospital in Brighton as a last chance to save his failing career. In truth, Jakub came from a very poor Polish family and had endured a tough, early start to his young life. Whilst working at the Royal London Hospital as a junior doctor, he had been juggling with two other jobs just to make ends meet. This had become increasingly more difficult, but he felt he had no choice because some of the extra income he earned in these positions, allowed him to send much- needed money back home to his family in Poland. As a result, he had performed badly in some of his studies, as well as during his hospital training and his performance as a junior doctor had most definitely suffered because of this extracurricular employment. His senior mentor at Whitechapel, Professor Michael Cotterall, knew of his hardships and seeing potential in the young man, the professor had pleaded his case for a second chance. It was the professor's pleas that had resulted in Kowalski being transferred to the Royal Sussex County Hospital in Brighton and given one last chance to save his vocation.

Since arriving in Brighton, Jakub had felt more comfortable in his inner self. He had always in his short life had his moments of quiet critical self-introspection, but following this recent relocation, he had grown in an awareness of self-worth and as a result, found a more secure personal inner happiness. This had been aided in no small part by his realising and his embracing of his sexuality as a gay young man. The close-knit gay community of Brighton was always renowned for being welcoming and friendly and Jakub had easily fitted in and found acceptance with those in the social group to which he had become attached. He also now, rather than working in several other jobs, had acquired a skill for obtaining various drugs from the hospital infirmary. He soon found these drugs he could easily sell, for recreational use, to a small group of his young homosexual friends in the bars he often frequented. This ability to get such drugs only added to his popularity amongst the group and it was an easy way for the young student doctor to top up his income, without working himself to death. His performance as a junior physician had bettered and he was well-liked at the local hospital by other junior staff. He was certainly above any suspicion of wrongdoing. His openly gay approach to life did raise an eyebrow or two with some of the more senior members of the hospital staff. But this flirting of his sexuality, although sometimes outrageous, was tolerated and most of his colleagues respected him for his much-improved attitude whilst at work.

Jack entered Compton Street and without hesitation stopped outside number thirteen. He pushed the shiny, silver key he held in his left hand up to his long fingers and inserted it into the pitted face of the old lock. Compton Street was made up of row-style houses, most of which were now modernised and very well maintained. Number thirteen stood out because it was so run down and badly neglected. The house had a sinister history, too. Legend had it that a female prostitute had been brutally murdered there many years before and that her body had been dreadfully mutilated by her attacker. The historic story also claimed that the police who attended the scene had searched for the woman's corpse but it had never been recovered. Perhaps unsurprisingly, given the gruesome nature of these events, rumours abounded that the dwelling was haunted by a disfigured old woman, reputed to be the ageing spirit of the victim. Indeed, many occupiers of the home had over the years, regularly claimed to have seen this female apparition and this had made the property virtually un-saleable, even in these more modern times.

Jack pushed open the front door and went inside the house, shutting the door gently behind him. Once inside, he found a welcoming warm fire lit in the grate of a very compact and barren lounge. The warmth from this fire, although inviting at first, had only helped to exacerbate the overall smell of dampness within the whole building and the scent of this stale moisture, clung to the heat in the air. Covering the old floorboards were very dated, heavily patterned carpets in places worn through and threadbare. There was only one downstairs window which was situated at the front of the lounge looking out onto the street. This window was adorned by net curtains which were tatty, matted and scrunched up, as well as being discoloured by age, mould and dirt. The windowpane itself was grimy and sullied and the window frame was in places rotten through, even from the inside.

Jack moved toward the window as if to check the curtains. However, instead of there being curtains pulled across it, there was an old threadbare rug that had been hung up to obscure the view of anyone attempting to look into the property from the street. He glanced at this and then turned away from it, having satisfied himself no one could see in.

The actual lounge furniture itself was sparse. It consisted of one tatty and shoddy old armchair. A pitted full-length mirror and a small rickety, woodworm infested, round table, onto which Jack placed the Gladstone bag he had clutched so protectively up until this point.

Exploring the ground floor, Jack discovered it had a small bare downstairs kitchen. Inside the kitchen, he found a heavily stained, solid wooden mahogany drainer. There was also a cracked and soiled white Butler sink with water dripping constantly from its aged taps. Jack ran one of the taps, then nodded in approval and turned it off again before leaving the room.

The last room downstairs, that Jack found, was off the kitchen and it was a make-do bathroom, which again smelt strongly of dampness and decay. Inside this bathroom, there was a cast enamelled bath that had not been used for years. It was covered with a lining of cobwebs and mould of varying putrid colours. There was also an ageing white soiled toilet and a small discoloured and heavily scratched ceramic sink. From the ceiling a single bare bulb hung in isolation from some twisted old-fashioned braided threadbare flex, this dusty bulb providing the only source of light within the room, there being no bathroom window.

Although extremely unwelcoming, these surroundings were strangely familiar to Jack, and as he slumped into the armchair in the lounge, he could be seen to relax. He had an aura of being settled. It was as if he had returned to an old home after a considerable period of absence.

Jack awoke with a start, the next morning, to the sound of the heavy Brighton traffic. Compton Street was a cut-through to the city centre and in the mornings the passing traffic made it noisy. This activity was unfamiliar to Jack and initially, it seemed to unnerve him. He had spent the night in the armchair and had not moved from where he had slumped there the night before. Now awake, he visibly gathered himself, standing up and brushing himself down. As he became more active he stretched and then caught sight of himself in the long lounge mirror, he stared intently at his reflection as if discovering a body he was not expecting to occupy.

Jack moved toward the window and feeling more ready to let in the daylight, he pulled at the rug which hung there and it dropped in a crumpled heap to the floor. The fire in the grate had all but burned out by this time and the damp property had a real cold early morning chill. On the small mantelpiece above the fireplace, Jack saw an envelope that he had not noticed the night before. The envelope looked out of place in the room, because it was clean and new. He reached out and took it from the mantelpiece and with the eagerness of a child tearing at a present he ripped it open and found a handwritten note inside it. It read …

Times have changed and so have the whores, but your infamy must prevail.
Terror and fear must reign once more, with the letting of blood.
In the master bedroom, there is the attire you will need. The leather wallet has much legal tender.
There are maps and details of their meeting places.
Happy hunting
Master Jack.

As instructed by the note, Jack left the lounge and went upstairs to the bedrooms of the neglected property. There were three bedrooms. One was a small box room and the door to this room was tilted and it hung lopsided, clinging to just one of the two rusty hinges that had once supported it fully. The upstairs hallway leading to all the bedrooms was devoid of carpet and the floorboards were pitted with woodworm and covered in a thick layer of grey dust. In the second bedroom part of the ceiling had come down in the room and broken laths and wet, damp, mouldy, fetid plaster littered the floorboards. Jack ignored this room and went straight into the master bedroom as the note had instructed.

The master bedroom as well as being very damp, was also quite bare. As with the rest of the house, any furniture present in the room was old and very minimal. There was no bed in this room, which increased its feeling of emptiness. A small dressing table stood against the far wall of the room and alongside this there was a very large wooden two-door wardrobe. The veneer on the wardrobe was very damaged and had been warped by the constant prevailing dampness. These features were obvious and depressing, to say the least, but Jack seemed oblivious to them and continued his exploration with enthusiasm and a sense of urgency.

Jack opened the old wardrobe door and inside it was surprisingly dry and well-kept with a variety of modern clothing; black roll-neck jumpers, some dress shirts, tee shirts and five pairs of men's denim jeans in a mixture of colours. There were also two long cashmere trench coats still on hangers and covered in clear polythene protectors; these coats were very smart and well-tailored. Also hanging from the rail in the wardrobe was a medium-sized modern leather-style man-bag, with strong shiny clasps and a long adjustable shoulder strap.

Jack now opened the other door of the wardrobe. Where he found an additional five shelves. The top two of which were filled with underwear, socks, and two black leather belts. He browsed these but gave them scant recognition. On the lower shelves which Jack seemed to be far more intrigued by, there was a smart black folder of paperwork, a ball of very rough coarse string and some large heavy-duty scissors. Beside these scissors, sat five very neatly folded, pristine, white, square cloths and a matching number of large men's material handkerchiefs. The handkerchiefs were also white, but were embossed in the corner with an ornate embroidered, black letter 'J'. There was also a box of new syringes and a box of long surgical-style gloves.

Jack, in seeing these latest items, shuddered violently, they clearly excited him. As this contortion subsided, he smiled demonically to himself. He now took out, and clutched to his chest the black folder from the wardrobe. He closed both of the wardrobe doors behind him and went quickly back downstairs.

On his return to the lounge, Jack sat himself down and settled into the tatty armchair. He then opened the popper on the folder and took out an amount of paperwork, which seemed to include hand-drawn maps with lists of places in the city. Inside the folder there was also an envelope, which contained a large amount of twenty-pound notes, neatly rolled in an elastic band. Jack immediately took the envelope and placed it into the drawer of the rickety table, which was next to his armchair. He then spent some time reading the paperwork he had found methodically and studiously. This occupied Jack for several hours, such was the intensity of the information and detail of the content that had been left for him.

The paperwork now studied and absorbed, Jack returned to the upstairs wardrobe. He picked up the ball of coarse string, the scissors, the box of surgical gloves and the box of syringes. These were all put to one side on the dressing table. He took one syringe from the newly opened box, a pair of surgical gloves and using the scissors cut two generous three-foot lengths from the ball of coarse string. Finally, he picked up a handkerchief and one square of the pristine white cloth.

All the while he was taking these items he was visibly struggling to contain his excitement. Closing the wardrobe door again Jack then returned to the lounge where he carefully placed all the items he had collected in the small drawers on the rickety lounge table. He sat down in the chair and shuddered violently.

"I must rest, not ready yet, not ready yet," he muttered quietly to himself.

CHAPTER THREE

Having rested up, Jack spent the next few nights exploring the places outlined on the maps he had found in the pouch in the wardrobe. All were gay bars or meeting places for gay men. His attire had changed; he had shaved off his moustache and thinned and toned down his previously bushy heavy sideburns. He was dressed in the modern clothing he had found left for him in his new place of residence. Jack now wore smart blue denim jeans, a black roll-neck jumper and one of the long cashmere trench coats. The only part of his outfit to remain unchanged was his highly polished black boots which were adorned with a bright ornate silver buckle. He cut the figure of an extremely handsome man, with a dark, full head of wavy hair and eyes as black as coal and in all the many bars he went into, he drew admiring casual glances from both men and women.

Jack respected his newness of being. He knew his transgressions through time initially left him physically weak. He realised he must concentrate on rebuilding his strength again quickly. So he rested in the mornings and never left Compton Street even in these early days until after lunchtime. Having explored several bars in the evenings, in the afternoons he familiarised himself with the town, visiting more of the meeting places outlined on the maps and in the written instructions that he had studied so dutifully. He also carefully worked out routes to and from Compton Street and structured a detailed map in his head of how to get back there safely if he were suddenly pursued or if he needed to escape unwarranted attention quickly.

After Jack had been in the city for five days he went out one evening scouting a new bar in the Brighton Lanes. He was fairly accustomed to the town and had a nagging eagerness to find victims and formulate a plan to aid with their demise. This new bar was packed mostly with gay young men who were clustered in couples and small groups; it was buzzing and the many men inside were effervescent and demonstrative. The atmosphere excited Jack even as he walked in. As he stood at the immaculately presented sparkling pink bar waiting to be served a drink he happened to overhear three men chatting at a nearby table. The three young men were talking openly about a new drug they had been using to enhance their sex lives. Two of them were quite graphic about their long-lasting effects. "Oh my God," one of the men squealed with an intensity of excitement. "It was so exhilarating; I can almost still feel it coming inside me!"

The three giggled. "I'm going to see Jakub," one of the men said. "And get some more, he's amazing." Jack was listening discreetly as he stood at the bar. The man's chatting continued, "He can get anything, anything you want." He extolled Jakub excitedly.

Jack now moved quite deliberately from the bar to the table. "Buy you guys a drink?" he said, his lustful black, piercing eyes staring at them with a dark licentious gaze.

"Ooh hello," one of the men said.

"Mind if I join you?" Jack added.

"No feel free," the liberal young men replied.

"More the merrier; not seen you in here before," one of them said.

"No, I'm new to the town and feeling my way

around so to speak," Jack said. "Let me get you guys that drink?" When Jack came back to the table from the bar, the three men were giggling and chatting once again. Jack, the man they only knew as a handsome dark stranger, had an almost irresistible charisma and they all instantly felt a stimulating magnetic attraction towards him. "I must be honest," he said as he put a tray of drinks down at the table and pulled up a chair. "I overheard you chatting, so you have a supplier for some recreational drugs?"

The three men had been drinking all evening and were well-plied with drink by this time. The gin and tonic coupled with the strange hypnotic draw of their new companion loosened their tongues, even to this new stranger. "I shouldn't really say this," the youngest of the three men said. "But as you are new in the city, I could help you out, perhaps in all ways," he smirked. He reached under the table and stroked Jack's leg right into his left groin. "Jakub," he went on. "Jakub, he's the boy who can get anything. Anything you want, for a price of course," he added and he winked devilishly at the black eyes gazing lustfully across the table at him. "He will be in here later. If you buy us another drink, handsome, perhaps I will introduce you."

Jack's secret agenda was unsuspected by the three men: his hideous murderous intent known only to him. Part of the stimulation he got from these pre-planned murders was the rush he felt drawing in and outwitting his unsuspecting prey. The thrill for Jack was in both the capture as well as the ultimate demise of his victims. Death excited him, but only when it was achieved by cunning and foresight.

To drug and thereby stupefy his victims had always

been his intent; he had used an injected drug to do just this in his killings at Whitechapel and by this unforeseen opportune moment, perhaps he had stumbled across a source for exactly what he sought. Things were going well and Jack was feeling very relaxed, he was tingling with excitement but it was controlled and to be enjoyed. In addition, the overwhelming tiredness he had felt after first arriving in the city was gone. Jack was showing all the cunning of a fox and he knew if things continued to go as well as they had to date, he would soon be ready to kill again.

True to the young man's words, Jakub Kowalski had come into the bar. "That's him," one of the men at the table said. "That's Kowalski, the tall handsome guy, with black eyes and dark wavy hair." Jack and Kowalski were remarkably similar in physical appearance and they easily could have been related. The three men made their initial introduction and Kowalski and his new acquaintance left the others at their table. The pair moved to a quiet corner at the back of the bar. Understandably, Kowalski was very cautious of the stranger and his motives at first but after an initial reticence, he also fell under his powerful hypnotic charm and opened up to him.

"So you're a student doctor?" the newly introduced stranger said to Kowalski. "I'm a medical man myself," he added. "And I'm after something special, something very special," he said. "If you can get it I can make you money. Real money! I've developed a recreational substance and just need this last drug to complete it."

Kowalski's face remained blank and dispassionate; he said nothing and was still being cautious, so Jack went on and without hesitation said, "Okay so I want Dizampathene, five phials of thirty-milligram strength if you can get them. I know you must have access to them and like I said, if you can get them, I will pay you serious money." Kowalski still did not reply his brain was spinning the proposition over. "Oh yes, and there is something else I need," Jack said. "I also need five phials of different men's blood."

Kowalski had said nothing to this point but this request for blood shook him from the hypnotic trance Jack seemed to have cast over him. He was shocked. "Drugs and blood no way, oh no way," he said. "I can get some drugs, but no I just can't get that. I can't," he added.

The young student doctor was familiar with Dizampathene. It is a synthetic version of the poison excreted on the back of a type of yellow-back tree frog, which was used for hunting by tribes in parts of Africa. The drug is a powerful suppressor of the nervous system, which slows the heart rate down to the extent of paralysing prey in seconds.

The frog's secretion does not kill outright, but gives the hunters the chance to catch up to and dispatch their helpless quarry. Its medicinal qualities had been extensively used after its discovery by Victorian doctors, who processed it and used it to treat spasms and fits. It was also used stronger doses, to disable mental health patients who were of a violent disposition.

Jack had injected it into his victims at Whitechapel to paralyse them and their vocal cords so they could not call out for help, but because of the lack of forensic science at that time, it had never been discovered in the victim's bodies. It was, however, the reason that their screams were never heard, something which in all of those historic murders had baffled the police.

In these more modern times, there was a new synthetic version of the drug, which was used mainly in lower doses to calm patients with mental health issues and those suffering from any form of chronic fitting, but this modern version Jack knew in a relatively strong dosage would work just as well for his evil purpose.

"I get the drug but why the blood?" Kowalski asked the stranger. "That's just odd," he added.

"It's the only way I can prove my drug. I need to prove the reaction in the blood itself," Jack whispered, his voice calm but emphatic. "If I can get the right substance you will have a recreational drug to blow the minds of your users and we can make a killing," he added. Jack's choice of words was quite considered and deliberate. "I have the cash," he said. "I'll give you whatever you want."

"I'm not so sure," Kowalski said.

"But you need the cash?" Jack replied.

Kowalski was being seduced by the hypnotic charisma of his seated companion. His first reaction of shock and of no way was he getting involved with this was changing. He thought he could not pass up the opportunity to make a large sum of money with just one deal. Jack knew he exuded a mesmerising aura and could see Kowalski's weakness and so pushed home his advantage.

"Look, I'll need an outlet for my new drug," he said to Kowalski. "It's a win-win situation for you. You can get paid for supplying me and when I have perfected the drug you can get paid for supplying the recreational users and I know you need the cash. Look this is it on the line," Jack said. "I was training to be a doctor like you, and I was struck off for one indiscretion. I know what I'm doing and how little you get paid. Don't miss this chance, it will set you up!"

Once again Jack's words were carefully and deliberately chosen. By now Kowalski had been completely taken in by this deception. He saw a familiarity in this stranger's situation to his own, something Jack had carefully engineered. *He's another doctor*, Kowalski thought to himself. *He must be trustworthy, he simply must be*, he thought.

Kowalski paused for a minute and then said. "Okay, I'll get it. I'll get what you asked for; give me two days." The two men agreed a price, Jack wasn't interested overly in the cost and the deal was done. "Meet you back here in two days at eight o'clock," Kowalski said and the two left the bar and set off in opposite directions. Jack smiled demonically to himself. It was far more than he could ever have hoped for. He went back to Compton Street, his gut knotted and his body rushed by adrenaline. He knew if Kowalski could acquire this ideal drug, his horrific murders and the ensuing suffering of his victims could finally begin.

CHAPTER FOUR

Two days had passed since Jack had met Kowalski for the first time. When he got to the bar where he had discovered his new drug-dealing friend, he saw Kowalski was already waiting for him outside. Jack was calm and exuded a blackness of aura even in these early days; Kowalski on the other hand was very nervous.

The young doctor knew what he was doing was very wrong, not only lawfully, but morally, too. His motivation was pure greed. Sadly not just selfish greed either, a lot of the extra money he made selling the drugs he stole from the hospital he sent back to help his family in Poland. It meant a great deal to them, as since he had moved to England his mother had become very ill.

"You made it then," Jack said. "Have you got my order?"

"Not here," said Kowalski in a timorous voice. Jack could see Kowalski's hands were shaking and his terror and the nervous way he was acting excited Jack and he had to control himself. He knew what that feeling led to. "Down here," Kowalski said. "Follow me," he added in a whisper. The pair walked a short way down Ship Street and into the start of the Lanes where it was secluded and quite dark. "Where is my money?" Kowalski said.

"It is here," Jack said. He reached into the inside of his long trench coat pocket and then handed the envelope to Kowalski. "There it is the five hundred pounds as you asked for."

"Okay and this is yours," Kowalski said as he took the small rucksack he was wearing from his shoulder. He opened it and took out a small brown bag with handles on it. Jack took the bag from him, and Kowalski hastily put the envelope into the rucksack.

"Do you not want to count it?" Jack said with a demonic smile. Kowalski's nervousness was exciting him to nearly a fever pitch.

"No, I can't here. I'll just have to trust you!" he said.

"As I will, you," Jack replied.

Kowalski paused for a moment and then said, "How will you contact me to sell the drug you make?" Although nervous, he knew there was far more money to be made if this new stranger's drug did as he said.

"I'll contact you at the hospital," Jack said knowing this would terrify Kowalski.

"No, not there, not ever there," Kowalski was desperate in his retort.

Jack had turned away from the panicked doctor. "Don't worry," he said. "I'll find you when I'm ready. After all, we are in this together all the way now." He walked away across the road, leaving Kowalski visibly shaking. Jack's words rang in Kowalski's ears.

Sat in the lounge of the house at Compton Street, Jack had a renewed sense of purpose about him. He carefully decanted the contents of his Gladstone bag, opened the drawer and took out two lengths of course string he had cut previously. He picked out a square of white linen cloth and removed one phial of the blood he obtained from Kowalski, and then placed all the items he needed into his man-bag.

Returning to the drawer he took out a handkerchief and this he placed in his left hand coat pocket. Jack performed every action quite methodically and deliberately; he was insane but organised. Finally, he unpacked a new syringe and taking one phial of the Dizampathene carefully filled the syringe with it. He then placed the syringe gently into his other coat pocket. He was ready. He gave a wry almost black smile and then a controlled shudder of exhilaration, as he closed the catch on the man bag and lifted it by its strap, placing it up and onto his right shoulder.

It was mid-afternoon when Jack came out of the house. The day was dull and overcast; it was not overly cold, but there was a strange half-lingering fog that started to appear as Jack stepped out from the property. He shut the door of the small row house and set off walking briskly down Compton Street. He went into Dyke Road, finally turning left into the long Queen's Road.

Focussed on his destination, Jack once again seemed oblivious to everything and everyone around him. Soon he was crossing the far end of the main Queen's Road and entering the large Brighton railway station. The station was not too busy at this time of day and Jack knew exactly the quarry he sought.

A young handsome man was leant up against the furthest back wall of the railway station, just at the far end of a small open plan café there. He was blonde, about twenty-five and dressed in a smart white tee shirt and black PVC trousers. His tee shirt did not quite cover his naval and he had a gold piercing in his clearly visible belly button. His trousers also finished above his ankles and he wore no socks, just patent black loafer-style shoes. He had a pink handkerchief protruding from his left front trouser pocket and this was hanging out loosely onto his trouser leg.

Jack had been told there was a young male

prostitute working at the train station. He knew he was blonde and also that he wore a pink handkerchief, which hung from his left trouser pocket. The handkerchief was a sign to those in the know that he was working. The young man had a regular clientele, usually married men.

The men were predominantly commuters, to whom he offered sexual services. They were thrill seekers who enjoyed him performing sex acts with them in various parts of the railway station, the thrill for the men being exaggerated by the risk of getting caught, there being in such a public place. It was a convenient stop for any prospective clients who could hop off a train, meet their companion and after a little fun continue on their journey. It was also a lucrative little business for the cash-needing prostitute.

Jack approached the young man; he knew that he used a code to recognise potential clients and that he should hang a white handkerchief from either the left-hand pocket of his coat or trousers to express his interest in the services the young man offered.

"You're not one of my regulars," the lad said.

"No," said Jack. "But you have been highly recommended, and I have the money. Can we go somewhere quiet?"

"It's fifty quid," the young prostitute said.

"Yes that's fine," said Jack, discretely showing the young man a large roll of twenty- pound notes.

"In or out then?" the lad said.

"Out," Jack replied.

"Okay follow me," the young man whispered. "But keep your distance, best we are not too obvious." The blonde young man went out of the side entrance of the station. He turned immediately right and right again down a narrow and dimly lit blind alley, which linked the railway station and the station yard behind it. The yard was surrounded by a wire fence coated in thick green plastic. The lad paused briefly as he went just inside the alley and tied his pink handkerchief to part of the fence. He then went a little further and pulled at a corner section of it, which opened slightly allowing him to pass into the yard. Jack followed shortly after and the lad helped him through the gap in the same fashion.

Once inside, Jack noticed that he and the young man were now standing in a large open plan, but covered, rear section of the railway yard. They were surrounded by numerous high stacks of various types of timber, which hid them completely from view on all sides. There were several used condoms scattered on the ground where the pair stood; this was a well-used venue.

"Strange this fog isn't it?" the young lad said. Jack said nothing and ignored the comment. "So anyway," he went on. "This is the maintenance yard for the station. We won't be bothered here. I've left my handkerchief on the fence, so the boys know I'm working. I don't share my customers!" He laughed. He had no clue of Jack's murderous intent for him and had presented himself like a lamb to the slaughter.

Jack asked the young man to turn around. "Let me look at you," he said. As the lad turned, Jack seized his opportunity. His black eyes raged as with a sudden movement he forced the balled-up white handkerchief that had been protruding from his coat pocket and rammed it forcefully into his victim's mouth to muffle his voice. Then, with his powerful frame, he overpowered the much smaller young man.

Without hesitation and with his free right hand Jack pulled the pre-prepared syringe from his coat pocket and plunged it deep into his victim's neck, simultaneously releasing the liquid inside. The syringe contained ten ml of the Dizampathene Jack had obtained the night before from Kowalski and the paralysing drug took only seconds to work. He held on to the lad firmly. Then gradually feeling the resistance against him reducing, he dropped his paralysed prey to the floor. His victim was fully conscious and aware of his situation, but because of the effects of the fast-acting drug, he just couldn't move or fight back.

Jack was in full murderous flight; he pulled savagely at the lad's clothing, ripping his tee shirt from him and dragging his trousers down from his recumbent body. Any cries for help by his conquest were muffled by the handkerchief in his mouth and the action of the drug which was paralysing his vocal cords.

Jack calmed again for a moment. He took his man-bag from his shoulder and placed it gently onto the ground next to his naked victim. Carefully, he opened the catch of the bag and removed the two long lengths of coarse string. He then, with more venom again, grabbed the young man's ankles one at a time, forcefully lifting them backward behind his knees and tying them tightly. With this action completed, he removed his victim's shoes and they fell simultaneously to the floor.

Jack picked up the shoes, studied them for a second, and then with great precision neatly placed them side by side, beside the lad's body. He turned his attention to the young man's hands and arms. Jack forced the limp limbs behind his conquest's back, viciously holding them in position and then bound these both tightly with the other piece of coarse string. His victim was trussed and helpless, his eyes staring fixated and glazed with fear. Jack knew there was no need to tie his victims because they were paralysed. He only bound them to add to their degradation and to emphasise their total helplessness.

With the first part of the attack completed, Jack removed his long trench coat and placed it neatly on one of the piles of timber, taking the time to fold it precisely. He knelt on the ground and carefully unpacked the man bag removing a piece of leather in the shape of a cylinder. This he untied and rolled out onto the cold concrete floor.

The leather roll contained pockets that housed an array of surgical instruments. It included varying types of scalpels, scissors and surgical cutting implements, which could be seen by both the attacker and his terrified captive. All of Jack's actions were premeditated, they were purposeful and insane.

From the man-bag Jack pulled the folded pristine white square cloth and the long pair of latex surgical gloves. He neatly unfolded the white cloth, placing it with precision on the ground and then stood up as he pulled the surgical gloves on. The whole procedure was well rehearsed, almost like a ritual and took only a few minutes.

"Now to you," he whispered gazing down at his bound and helpless captive.

Jack removed the balled-up handkerchief from his victim's mouth. The Dizampathene by this time had completely paralysed the young man's vocal cords and he was quite unable to cry out or speak. Jack took the handkerchief and put it into the man- bag. "That's better," he said in demonic fashion.

"Please call out for help if you wish," he added in a taunting voice. He knew full well his victim was quite unable to do so.

Jack pulled the young man up, resting his back on a pile of wood behind him. Without another word, he took the smallest scalpel from the roll of instruments. With the precision of a surgeon he stroked and then removed both his helpless victim's pert nipples. He leaned over and placed the nipples symmetrically onto the crisp white cloth that he had laid on the floor.

The young victim's eyes watered with the intense pain of this brutality and a salty tear ran down his cheek, but he was still unable to speak or cry out. Jack then calmly and without any expression of feeling replaced the small scalpel in the bag and, showing no mercy, he took the largest surgical blade from the leather roll. He grabbed at his victim's hair and forcefully pulled his head forward.

"I want you to watch this," he whispered, in a depraved and manic tone. Purposefully, he drove the blade into the young man's flesh just below his sternum and ran it down the entire length of his body, to the top of his pelvic area.

At first, because of the sharpness of the blade, this wound did not open; it seemed to take a few seconds for the flesh to register it was cut and then as the elasticity of the skin was broken, it sprang apart. The wound bled very little at this time, as the side effects of the Dizampathene slowed the heart rate so drastically and also coagulated the blood of the victim it was injected into.

Jack reached out and viciously pushed one hand into the gaping wound; he gripped the exposed sausage-like intestines he found inside, pulling them forward and laying them on the stomach and chest of his young victim, who was still conscious and being forced to watch as he was being gutted.

Jack's eyes blackened again, almost as if he was feeding off the energy of the suffering he was inflicting. Lifting his heavily bloodied glove from the open wound, he violently pulled his victim's hair, this time forcing his head back and exposing the full surface area of his throat. Jack raised the blade of the large scalpel gripped by his other gloved hand so it was directly in the view of his helpless conquest. He then lowered it suddenly, driving it deeply into the neck of his trembling prey just below his right ear.

Jack brutally twisted the scalpel several times and then with a forceful jagged cutting motion, he ran the sharp blade viciously across the exposed throat ripping through skin, flesh, arteries and sinews. This act was so violent that it caused the cartilage in his captive's throat to make a pitiful cracking sound, as it split under the duress of the incision. The wound, although deep, held together for a moment and then gaped open. Pitifully the young man could be heard making a weak gasping noise, as air was released, but not able to return to his lungs.

Jack's murderous lust was still not satisfied; all his earlier calmness was gone and he was now frenzied. With one scything motion, he forced his blade down into his victim's groin. Once there he removed the young man's genitals, holding them aloft in his hand like a trophy, before forcing them into his victim's open mouth. This he did with such pressure that the tip of his victim's penis could be seen at the back of his throat, through the exposed gaping wound across his neck.

Jack shook violently. His conquest was dead and the crazed frenetic killer seemed to revert to his prior calm self, almost as if the depraved madness driving him had left his being. He wiped the blade of the large scalpel on the dead young man's body and placed it back into the leather roll. Once more he removed the smallest scalpel from its pocket, this time quite deliberately using it to cut five single straight vertical lines into his victim's face on the left cheek.

Jack took a deep breath; he had killed but still had more work to do. He reached into the man bag again, this time removing one of the plastic phials of blood he had purchased from Kowalski and a small folded-up piece of paper, which he put carefully to one side of the corpse, resting some flesh on it to hold it in place under the lifeless body. The torso of his victim was nearly unrecognisable as a human being, but Jack was not finished with it.

Still knelt beside the corpse, Jack carefully removed one of his gloves and placed it on the ground near to wear his victim's hands were tied. He picked up the phial of blood and poured a small amount of it into the palm of the glove as it lay on the ground. With great precision, he then lifted the lad's still-bound right hand and with a dragging motion, he scraped it through the blood on the glove, ensuring some of it was forced up and under the fingernails.

Finally, and almost as an afterthought, Jack noticed a used condom next to the body; he picked it up and with his gloved hand, smeared the semen contents from it onto the right facial cheek of the severely mutilated torso.

His awful work here was nearly done. Jack removed the second glove from his hand and then gently as if nurturing something precious to him, rolled up the leather pockets holding his instruments of death. He tied up the cylindrical roll and gathered up the gloves, small blood phial and the empty syringe from the ground, and placed them in the man bag before fastening it shut.

Jack seemed immune to the carnage which lay before him. The effects of the Dizampathene in the body of the corpse had started wearing off and all of the hideous wounds were leeching blood, much of which was as dark as the eyes of the creature that had inflicted them.

Jack reached out, picked up his coat and put it on calmly, just as one would if going out on an everyday walk. The long heavy trench coat covered the many splatters of blood on his clothing. Putting his man bag on his shoulder and without looking back he climbed through the hole in the fence from which he had previously entered. He walked past the pink handkerchief, paused, glanced and smiled at it demonically and then went out into the street. With great cunning, he knelt on one knee at the entrance to the dark alley, as if he had been walking past and just stopped there to tie a shoelace. Doing this gave him a chance to look quickly around and check no one was there to see him leaving the scene of his depraved act.

The fog had all but gone and satisfied the coast was clear Jack stood up and calmly walked away. His whole murderous act had taken just forty minutes and now he was safely on his way back to the security of Compton Street.

CHAPTER FIVE

Two uniformed police officers stood outside the cordoned-off yard at the back of the Queen's Road railway station. A white incident tent could be seen to have been erected inside. The scene was a hive of activity, everyone behind the cordon wearing white forensic suits and masks and there was lots of coming and going. A car pulled up and out got two suited men, who stood out as policemen as sure as if they were in uniform. One of the men was Detective Chief Inspector Tim Martin.

Martin had been on leave and had been called back to duty at the request of the station commander, because of the serious nature of this latest incident. Martin was an experienced detective and in his twenty-four years on the job had seen most things. He was a hard man, very opinionated and sometimes unorthodox. He had worked his way up through the ranks and hated the 'Bramshill' and fast-tracked officers, so common now in the modern job.

His arrogance and lack of political correctness at times disturbed his seniors and he was sometimes considered tyrannical by those he was senior to. But despite this, he was an excellent detective and all both above and below him in rank respected him for this.

The man with him was his good friend Sergeant John Carter; the two had joined the job together and worked well as a team. They had both worked together on several high-profile murder cases in Brighton and were known to get results. Both men went behind the cordon and put on their forensic attire. Martin led the way into the tent and despite his years of experience was visibly shocked by the sight of the disembowelled torso that greeted him. Mary Marshall, the division's top pathologist was already inside the tent and standing over the body.

"Hello, Tim," she said. "This one's not pretty, I'm afraid." Sergeant Carter had followed Martin into the tent, and he too was visibly shocked at the state of the corpse. "We've got pictures," Marshall said. "And I've had a preliminary look at the body. I'd say he's been dead for around fifteen hours looking at him. He was found by the yard manager when he opened up at six this morning."

"Anyone know who he is?" Carter asked.

"Yes," Marshall said. "The yard manager thinks it's a young male prostitute called Toby Clarke. He and a few other young men of the same vocation use the yard to entertain their 'pick-ups'. I'm not jumping to any conclusions, but I'm sure that is semen on his right cheek, so it fits."

"Careless," the sergeant muttered.

"Let's hope so for our sake," Martin replied. "We will need that fast-tracked, Mary. If it's our killer's, we need a monster like that off the streets now." Both Martin and Marshall had been doing their jobs too long to leap to any assumptions. They knew murder scenes had a strange habit of not being anywhere near as obvious as they first seemed.

"There is more," Marshall said. "Next to the victim, we found this note. The forensic guys have dusted it for fingerprints but there are none on it. But it seems that our killer is a poet of sorts," she added.

"What do you mean?" Martin asked.

"Well here is the note, handwritten," she said.

"Read it."

Martin opened the blood-stained note that had been folded the way it was found. His gloved hands fumbled with it in his enthusiasm to get to the writing inside in the hope it was a vital clue to any potential killer's identity. He lifted it up and read it out loud.

> "They'll not protect nor do they care,
>
> My gift to you this truth I share,
>
> I walk your streets upon my stealth,
>
> But an apron of leather, prefer myself."

"Leather apron?" Carter said. Unsure what the final line was meant to reveal.

"Yes," Marshall replied quickly. "That's what they used to call, 'Jack the Ripper'."

"A lunatic, that is what this killer is," Martin said sharply. Focussed again, Martin sighed. "Right let's get back to 'the nick', John. I'll leave it with you, Mary. I do need that autopsy report as soon as possible please."

"Yes okay, Tim. I'll get the body moved and do the autopsy as a priority on my return to the morgue. I'll ring you when I'm done."

The two officers stepped from the incident tent. Both seemed visibly relieved to no longer be in the presence of the mutilated corpse. "Let's get a handwriting expert on this note, John. It's something more to go on and we need to find whose semen that is!" As they removed their forensic outfits, Martin looked at his sergeant. "Right, priorities are that we need to get a statement from the yard manager, confirm the identity of the victim and get someone up here to look at the railway station closed circuit television. It may, if we are lucky, have picked up images of our killer with Clarke if that is who the victim is. We need to try and keep a lid on this, John. I've got a very bad feeling about this one, my old friend," he added. "I'm going back to 'the factory', I need to get everything up and rolling as soon as possible, the time is already getting on. I'll see you there, okay?"

Back at the John Street police station, the C.I.D. floor was having its large briefing room converted into a temporary major incident suite when Martin got back. Four detectives had already been assigned to the case by the C.I.D. duty inspector, two were setting up the incident room and Sergeant Carter had organised for the other two of them to go to the station railway yard, where they were taking a statement from the yard manager.

Martin took some time organising himself for an initial briefing of his detectives and then liaised with the duty C.I.D. inspector. "You have four of my best people, sir," the C.I.D. inspector said to Martin. "And D.C.s Hopkins and Thompson are already at the railway station following a request from Sergeant Carter and they are getting a statement from the yard manager as we speak. From now on it's all yours and best of British," the duty inspector added. "We are swamped with our workload."

"Right, John," Martin said to his skipper who had just got back to the police station and grabbed a cup of lukewarm, very insipid-looking tea, from the corridor vending machine. "Contact Hopkins and Thompson at the railway station and make sure they pick up the surveillance C.C.T.V. tapes from the main train station office. Oh yes and ask them to liaise with the British Transport Officers there. We could do with some background on the way these prostitutes are working on the railway station and get them to see if they know the lad Toby Clarke and any of his regular clients," he added.

"I have already spoken to the British Transport Officers before I left the scene, governor," Carter replied. "They have formally now identified Clarke as the victim. They are getting a report together for you on known associates etc."

"Oh well done, John. Right, who are the other detectives we have on the case?

"D.C. Dave Smith and D.C. Becky Thomas, they are setting up the incident room sir."

"Okay, once they finish that, I will get them on tracing the young victim's family and when D.C. Hopkins and D.C. Thompson get back I want a meeting with everyone on the case in the major incident room. I'm going up there now to take over from Dave and Becky. I'll give them their duties and do some more prep for the initial briefing. Once you've told the two officers at the railway station yard what we want them to do come and join me there, John. Then we will get everyone together and do the full case briefing when they are back at 'the nick'."

With that Martin's phone rang and he glanced at it. "It is Marshall's office," he said. "Wait a minute, John, this could be important."

He paused for a moment to place some papers down on the desk and then took the call. After a quick chat with the pathologist, he put down the phone and looked at his waiting sergeant. "Marshall wants to see us, John. Change of plan then. Okay, we will tell the troops what we want them to do for now and then we will go to the morgue. We will do the full briefing when we get back. Oh and let's tell them all to ring home, this could be a late one, early turn or not, no one is going home at two p.m. today."

Martin and Sergeant Carter arrived at the morgue. It was only a short car ride from the police station and situated on Brighton's Lewes Road. Inside they found Marshall. "Good timing," she said. "I've just finished my basic preliminary autopsy and got some initial D.N.A. results for you, Tim. You are not going to like them."

The three stood in front of the mangled wreck of the corpse which lay on a trolley in front of them. "Right," Marshall went on. "Firstly, our victim has now been formally identified by British Transport Police, as I believe you know now, Tim. He is, as was suggested at the crime scene, Mr. Toby Clarke and it was semen as I expected on the victim's face. We have matched the D.N.A. from the semen on the database. It is that of a police officer, a P.C. Josh Earl."

"Oh, shit no," Martin said. "That's all we bloody need!"

"Well," Marshall said. "It was bound to flag up; we have all the officer's D.N.A. samples on file to eliminate them from crime scenes. Sadly, for Earl, this one's incriminating him at this time, but that's your department, Tim, I can only give you the facts as I have them. That aside, there is more D.N.A. evidence," the pathologist said. "There was blood which was not either the victim's or Police Constable Earl's under the right hand fingernails of the corpse. We are working on this but have no matches yet; it could be that the victim scratched his attacker."

"What about the time of death?" Martin asked.

"We have narrowed it down to around sixteen to seventeen hundred hours on Wednesday afternoon. So when Clarke was found he had been dead for around fifteen hours. It gets worse," she said. "The victim was drugged before being killed; we found a needle puncture mark under some of the ripped flesh on his neck and our fast-track drug analysis has revealed traces of Dizampathene in his blood. Not exactly an everyday drug," Marshall added. "But it shows up quite clearly because it's synthetic."

"You said synthetic, a synthetic what?" Martin quizzed the pathologist.

"A manmade substitute drug for the real thing," she said.

"So if he was drugged, at least perhaps the poor lad didn't feel anything when he was being mutilated?" Carter said.

"I'm afraid it doesn't work like that," Marshall went on. "Dizampathene attacks and paralyses the body; it stops the signals to the brain relating to both limb and muscle movements, but it doesn't block pain receptors. No," she said. "The young man would have felt everything; every wound," she added.

"Phew," Martin said puffing out his cheeks "In what order were the wounds inflicted?"

Marshall moved toward the corpse as if to demonstrate the awful sequence of events. "Well," she said. "It looks, and I still need to confirm this, that after being drugged the victim was tied up. I can only surmise that this action was performed purely to add to his degradation because he would have been already paralysed by the Dizampathene. No specifically identifiable knots or types of string were used to bind the limbs. The nipples, it appears, were removed first and these were skilfully and deliberately taken with a very sharp blade. He was then cut from the base of the sternum. This time the incision was made with a larger blade, again, very sharp I would say. A large surgical scalpel most probably, this wound was deliberate and precise and ran from the sternum over the abdomen and finished at the top of the pelvic area. Part of the intestines were pulled from this wound and laid onto the chest and stomach."

"Surely the victim would be unconscious by now and his attacker would be covered in blood – the bleeding must have been intense?" Martin said.

"Sadly, no on both counts," Marshall replied. "These wounds were made with such sharp blades that the body would take time to register them. No, he was conscious whilst he was being gutted."

"And the bleeding?" Carter said.

"Well, Dizampathene dramatically slows the heart rate down and in addition has as a side effect of coagulating the blood. The bleeding would have occurred but not in any great profusion; the attacker would have splatters at most," Marshall replied. "And next," she went on. "The attacker cut the victim's throat, and from the wound size and shape, the same cutting tool that opened the abdomen was used. This time, however, the attack was more frenzied, more frantic. The cut was made with a huge amount of force. It is such a deep and penetrating wound it has shattered all the cartilage in the throat. You both look a little shocked. Do you need a moment?"

"No, no," the two men replied.

"Let's just get this over. But it is not just a Friday night stabbing is it," Martin said.

"Right then," Marshall said. "The attacker then used the same large blade and removed the victim's genitals. Similarly, this wound was inflicted savagely. The genitals having been removed were then violently forced into our victim's mouth. Again, this was done with such force that his mouth split open on both sides of the oral cavity, but by this point, I would say he was at least unconscious and most probably dead. The brutality of such an act I'm afraid I have no words for," she added. "Oh, and one more thing, did you notice the five vertical lines carved into the left cheek on his face when you were at the crime scene?"

"Yes," Martin said, "another calling card?"

"I'm afraid so," Marshall replied. "After the madness of these catastrophic wounds the killer inflicted, he used a small scalpel to cut these quite exactingly into the face, some sort of ritual symbol perhaps. At this time, I cannot be sure when this act was undertaken. Looking at the wound I would be inclined to think after death, but I need to confirm that and indeed the order of all the wounds inflicted in the full autopsy report. And something off the record, Tim," Marshall said. "I think whoever did this must have some sort of medical knowledge," her voice troubled for the first time.

"Like a doctor?" Martin enquired.

"Well, I wouldn't be that definite, but it's someone who knows about human anatomy and has some skills in using surgical instruments. In addition, Dizampathene is a specialised drug, it's not something you can just buy off the shelf and is only found in hospitals in the main. Anyway, I'll complete the full autopsy and have the analytical written report for you by four o'clock today. That's as much as I can tell you for now."

"Thanks for being so quick," Martin said.

"It is the wonders of modern science. Oh, and the D.N.A. database," she added. "I'll say one thing, though. Whoever did this, needs to be caught and quickly. This was an awful murder and particularly brutal." She paused for a moment and then with a devious delivery said, "Almost Ripper-like!" And she turned away from the two men and went into her small office.

CHAPTER SIX

After the killing, Jack returned to the security of Compton Street. He was exhausted from his murderous exploits. Once inside the house he removed his coat and let it just fall to the floor. The sanguinary butchery was over and had left his clothing covered in splatters of blood, but Jack showed no interest in removing it or changing at this time.

Instead, he collapsed into the small lounge armchair and his body gave a violent and sudden, almost fit-like shudder. With this spasm finished he gazed vacantly at the ceiling for a few minutes. "I must rest, must rest," he muttered to himself in a muted voice and he closed his eyes as he slipped into a recumbent stupor.

When Martin and Sergeant Carter got back to the John Street police station, D.C. Hopkins and D.C. Thompson had also returned. The two detective constables stood chatting to D.C. Smith and D.C. Thomas.

"Right," Martin said. "Everyone in the major incident room; let's see what we have got." Martin then turned to his sergeant. "John, before you come and join us, would you find out what P.C. Earl was doing at the time of the murder, whether he was working or on rest days? Then tell the communications room to locate P.C. Earl and get a uniformed mobile unit to pick him up. I want him found and brought into the station."

"Yes, of course, sir."

"Get them to put him in my office and he is not to be left alone until I get there. We will see him once I've completed the briefing." Martin then disappeared into his own office to get a few items of paperwork, when he reappeared Sergeant Carter was coming back down the corridor. "What's the news on Earl?" Martin said.

"He is currently on a rest day, governor. The duty roster appears to show he was working on the town centre patrol team and was doing a ten a.m. until six p.m. shift on the day of the murder, but I'm waiting for that to be confirmed. We are still trying to establish if he is at home currently. But I have made sure that the Rottingdean car is on stand-by to pick him up, once we have verified his location."

"Good John. Right, let's get on with this briefing."

The temporary major incident room had been laid out with three whiteboards in front of a single row of six chairs. Martin and Sergeant Carter stood at the front as all the other detectives found themselves a seat. There was a knock at the door and two more detectives came in. It was nearly two p.m. by this time, and these two detectives had been told to go and join Martin's team by the C.I.D. duty inspector, as they turned up for their late turn, two until ten p.m. shift. "Inspector Simmons thought you could do with us," the taller of the two detectives said as the pair took out another couple of chairs.

"Yes, come in and sit down," Martin replied.

All the detectives in the room knew one another and uttered a few quick hellos. Martin addressed them all. "Okay settle down," he said. The two new detectives were D.C. Andrews and D.C. Fuller, both experienced officers who had worked with Martin before.

"Okay so our sequence of events is this," Martin said. He was writing on one of the whiteboards. "Our victim is one Toby Clarke, he was twenty-four years old and we know he was working at the railway station as a prostitute. He was found dead on Thursday at six a.m. in the yard at the back of the railway station. He had been dead according to the pathology team since between sixteen and seventeen hundred hours on the Wednesday afternoon. He had some blood deep under the fingernails of his right hand, which could be possibly that of attackers and some semen on his face. Marshall the pathologist is working on these. We know this yard is used by several young male prostitutes.

We have been liaising with the British Transport Police and they have provided us with a full written report of Clarke's associates, known friends etc. You all have a copy of this report in your individual paperwork trays. Clarke's body had been severely mutilated." By this point, Sergeant Carter had put up a row of pictures of the body from the scene. Martin moved over to them. "The wounds are quite horrific and significant," he said. "The pathologist's report will outline them to you. You will all be given a copy of this too. These details are important; this is not just a casual stabbing.

There is something else as well that stays just in these four walls," Martin said. "Near the victim, there was a note, we have it here. No fingerprints were found on it, but it does have a historical reference to 'Jack the Ripper'." A ripple of whispers went around the room. "We are going to get a handwriting analysis, if for nothing else, to give us a clue if our killer is left or right-handed. A copy of the note is on the whiteboard, I suggest you all read it," he added.

"Another lunatic," Sergeant Carter interjected.

"Yes," Martin said. "But nothing about this must get out to the press, or all hell will break loose! Okay moving on, we know from D.C. Thomas that our victim has no known family and had been in care until he was eighteen years old. I will leave it with you Becky to follow up on friends, fellow prostitutes and anyone else who knew the victim. We need a more detailed profile of his contacts."

"Okay, sir."

"Has anyone viewed the railway station C.C.T.V. footage yet?" Martin asked.

"Yes, sir," replied D.C. Tony Hopkins. "Both myself and D.C. Thompson viewed it in 'the nick' C.C.T.V. suite. It's a strange one, sir," he went on. "The victim appears clearly on it. He is leaning against the back wall of the railway station and he looks as if he is talking to himself. He then leaves the station and goes out of sight."

"What not with anyone?" Carter interjected. The sergeant's voice showed disbelief.

"No, skip, we saw no one talk to him, or leave with him. We found that odd!"

"Was he talking on a phone?" Martin said.

"No, definitely not, sir" Hopkins added. "He did not seem to have a phone with him and the way he was dressed, if he had a phone, we would have definitely seen it and certainly noticed if he answered it."

Martin puffed out his cheeks again. "Okay, so we need to establish how and when he met his killer. I want you two to go back up to the railway station. Put up boards inside and out asking for witnesses and quiz anyone who works on the platform; someone must have seen something. Okay, you guys that have just joined us." Martin addressed the two late turn detectives D.C. Andrew and D.C. Fuller. "Clarke our victim was drugged before he was attacked. The drug used was a substance called Dizampathene. Marshall says it's not a common drug and is quite specialised in its use. We need to find out how our killer got hold of it. Try the city hospitals and check to see if there have been any burglaries at local pharmacies recently. We need to find who manufactures the drug and who they supply it to. Sergeant Carter and I are going to follow up on the two D.N.A. leads Marshall got from the victim. These are our best shots at a lead on our potential killer at this time. One last thing I must stress, we have kept the press at bay on this one up until now I'd like to keep it that way, no casual 'chit chat' to anyone about this, okay?

Right fill your boots, people you know what you have to do, get on it. We will meet here for a quick de-brief at eighteen hundred hours then call it a day. You new lads you'll be on until twenty-two hundred hours, so you can pick up on any jobs that don't get done, so make sure you're here for the eighteen-hundred-hour de-brief too. Leave me a list of anything you do after we have gone home in my in-tray. I'll clear it with Inspector Simmons so you can come in at seven in the morning and pick up on the twelve-hour shifts with us from then on. Okay?"

"Yes, sir, that's fine."

"And welcome to the overtime!" D.C. Smith said, with a smile.

"Yes there will be loads of that I fear," Martin replied.

There was a little rumbling of chat as the detectives pushed their chairs back and made their way out of the briefing room. Sergeant Carter went over to Martin and when they were alone in the room said. "You didn't tell them about Earl, sir?"

"No, John," Martin said. "Let's get our facts right

before we let any cats out of the bag on that one. Can you go and see if they have confirmed he was working at the time of the murder? I'm going to go along to the C.C.T.V. suite in the 'Whisky Victor' control room and watch that video footage from the railway station. I just want to be sure nothing has been missed. I just cannot believe we do not see who Clarke walks off with. Meet me in there John when you have found out about P.C. Earl, will you?"

"Yes, of course, governor."

Martin went down to the designated C.C.T.V. suite, and once inside he got one of the control room P.C.s to find the C.C.T.V. tapes from the railway station for him. Martin played all the tapes several times, but his detective constables were correct. The young prostitute could be seen to be talking and he even gestured several times, but there was no one on the tape whom he appeared to be talking to. It was just as if he was talking to himself.

Martin went back to the incident room, but he was still thinking about the tapes. Sergeant Carter returned himself to the incident room only a few minutes later, and he had a big smile on his face.

"I missed you in the C.C.T.V. suite, governor," he said. "They said you had already come back here. But it's fucking good news as far as P.C. Earl is concerned, governor," he said. "Josh Earl was working; in fact, he had a prisoner at eleven a.m. on the Wednesday when Clarke was killed and he spent all day at 'the nick' processing and interviewing her, as the minor crimes unit was so busy. And he was not alone," the sergeant went on, "because his prisoner was a female, he had a female officer, a P.C. Sands with him all day. It was a complicated case. He never left 'the nick' and they didn't get off duty until twenty-one hundred hours. He can't be our killer!"

"Oh, that is good news, John. Well, for him certainly. Yes, and I watched those tapes again and Hopkins and Thompson are right. The young lad Clarke looks as if he is talking to himself, or a fucking ghost," Martin said.

Carter could see this was troubling his senior officer. "Forget the tapes for now, governor, let's see Earl first. He should be here in an hour or so." he said.

Josh Earl was now waiting for Martin and Carter in the chief inspector's office; it had taken some time to establish his whereabouts and to get him picked up and brought back to the police station. The young constable had an anxious look on his face. He knew something was seriously wrong if he had been pulled back to the police station on his rest days. It was not a routine thing for any officer to be picked up by a patrol car and brought back to 'the nick'. Martin and Sergeant Carter went into the office and Sergeant Carter shut the door. "You are a lucky boy," Martin said. The pair relayed the sequence of events that had led to him being brought in. Earl was visibly shocked when told his semen had been found on the face of the victim of a murder at the local railway station. Martin described Clarke to the young police constable, if nothing else in the hope he might know something more about him. "I've never been with that lad," Earl said. "I have seen him there a few times, but he's not my type."

"But you have been at the scene; what the fuck do you think you are playing at?" Carter said.

Earl broke down. "I paid a lad for sex there on Monday night at about eight in the evening, but it wasn't the victim, I swear it," he added.

"We will need a statement from you," Martin said. "And you are suspended. This is still a serious matter." Turning to his sergeant, he said. "Right, let's go and de-brief the troops, update them with what we have got and then it's time we went home, John. We will function so much better with something to eat and a little rest."

CHAPTER SEVEN

The next morning, Martin arrived early for his shift as he invariably did. His devotion was to the job he loved; in fact, he had been divorced now for several years as his marriage could not flex with his workload and he was aptly described by his Sergeant John Carter at a recent party they attended together, as married solely to 'the job'. Underneath his often brash exterior, though, he was a thoughtful, intelligent man, who worried about getting things right and getting justice for the victims of the crimes he worked on. "Morning, governor," John Carter said as he walked into his senior officer's office with a cup of weak underwhelming tea from the machine in the corridor for them both.

"Morning John," Martin sighed. "I wonder what today holds for us?" he added his voice a little fraught. "That young lad we discovered yesterday. That shocked me."

"Yes, and me, governor," Carter replied.

Slowly the six detectives on the case turned up for duty and assembled in the incident room for the daily morning briefing. In most police investigations there have been events that have unfolded during the night. In this case, a detailed autopsy report had been finished by Marshall and had been sent over to the detective chief inspector's computer, which confirmed the awful sequence of events that everyone in the case was now aware of. In addition, there were several other reports from British Transport Police, who had only come on duty later in the day of the killing and had come up with additional contacts for the victim Clarke. These would have to be followed up over the next few days. All the detectives were busy collating information and tracing associates of the young dead prostitute. Further reports came into Martin from the forensics teams; unusually there was no additional D.N.A. evidence found at the scene of the murder and although the detectives were busily building a comprehensive profile of the young prostitute's habits and daily life, the case was stagnating in a continuance of dead ends. As yet Martin had not found a motive for the killing, which played intensely on his mind.

It was a little after two fifteen on Saturday afternoon when Jack was to leave the house at Compton Street again. He walked calmly but quickly along the road, his man bag hanging loosely from his shoulder. He left Dyke Road and walked down North Street in the direction of the Old Steine and once there changed direction again, now heading towards the Brighton Palace Pier and the seafront. The streets were busy but Jack remained just another face in the crowd.

Once Jack reached the pier, he mounted the pavement and walked toward the Lower Esplanade, his long strides now ate up the ground as he got nearer and nearer to the focal point of his journey. Jack was nearly a quarter of the way along the Lower Esplanade of the seafront. He had left the crowds of people behind. It was a cold damp afternoon and a hazy fog had inexplicably started to descend on the seafront, which was quiet and, apart from the one odd-looking old man he passed on his route, almost deserted.

Jack's destination was to be Duke's Mound. Dukes Mound is a hilly embankment that links Brighton's Lower Esplanade and the main Coast Road, culminating at the Brighton Marina. The embankment overlooks the sea and the beach. It is heavily planted with thick bushes, which if one leaves the pathways that run through it at various gradual gradients, give perfect cover to those persons wishing to perform acts of a sexual nature outside with one or more partners. It is a well-used venue and well-known to the local police, as are the public toilets which back onto it about halfway along the embankment stretch of Marine Parade and in the direction of the main marina itself.

Jack paused for a minute as he reached his intended destination. He felt inside his left coat pocket and pulled at the white handkerchief, removing it just enough to remain exposed.

He had done his research and knew there was a young male prostitute working the Lower Esplanade toilets. Jack also knew that the handkerchief showing from his left-hand pocket would identify to the young man that he had an interest in the sexual services the prostitute offered.

Jack continued on his journey again and within seconds he could see the figure of a young man leaning against the side of the gentleman's public toilet at the bottom of the Esplanade. As Jack walked closer his eyes which had been glazed and focused to this point could be seen to blacken. They became almost transfixed on the outline of the young man at the toilets, concentrated like that of a lion about to chase down prey and make a kill. The lad looked up, drew a drag from the cigarette he was smoking and flicked the tar-stained butt out into the road. He glanced at the handkerchief hanging from Jack's left pocket. "You looking for me and some fun?" he said to Jack as he pulled at the pink handkerchief hanging from his own right-hand trouser pocket, which was the sign he was working.

"Yes," Jack said.

"It's fifty quid," the young lad said. "You got the money?" Then smiling at Jack he went on. "Handsome aren't you, makes a nice change," he added.

Jack showed the young man a large roll of twenty-pound notes held together by an elastic band.

"In the bog or the bushes then, how do you want me?" the lad retorted.

Jack stood transfixed for a moment; he was almost shaking with blood lust. He drew a small breath and looked into the young man's eyes. "Bushes," he said.

The smartly dressed lad stood up and stepped away from the wall of the toilet; he was in his early twenties and wore tight, light blue jeans and a figure-hugging, immaculately pressed white tee shirt. He ran his hands up through his dark curly hair as he made eye contact again with Jack. He smiled briefly once more. "Follow me then, lover," he said, and he walked up to the small path that took the pair up into the heart of the mound and onto what would be the killing ground.

By now it was nearly quarter to three in the afternoon and the ever-thickening fog was ignored by both men as they left the main footpath and went through two large bushes, which opened up to a square of flat earth. The square was well-trodden and in the middle of it, there were two strategically placed paving slabs. This area was well known to the prostitute and well used pretty much exclusively by him, as he had discovered it and cleared it of some of the bushes to make it a little more open and accessible. "We are secluded here," the young man said and he moved forward towards Jack, opening his arms as if to remove

Jack's coat.

Jack ignored the gesture and stared at him again. "I want you gagged and helpless. It's my thing," Jack said coldly.

"You're paying. You can have what you want. I'm bound to please," the lad grinned. "So, you want to be rough? Okay, but no bruises." He laughed. "If you mark me it's extra."

"On your knees," Jack said and as the young man did as he was asked, Jack reached in and took out the white handkerchief that had previously been hanging partially from his coat pocket. The lad who was now kneeling was staring into Jack's groin and stroking his clients' thighs. "Look up at me," Jack said. As the young prostitute raised his head, quite suddenly and without any warning, Jack violently pushed the balled-up white handkerchief into his victim's open mouth.

Oddly the young man was not initially too alarmed by this aggressive action, many of his clients had kinky preferences and he took this as just a norm of this particular client. Things changed rapidly, though, as Jack reached into his left-hand coat pocket, where he took hold of the loaded syringe he had previously placed inside it. With one swift motion, he pushed the coat forward, driving the needle through his coat and into the kneeling young man's neck. Holding the back of his victim's head tightly with his right hand, he emptied the syringe into his captive. The lad tried to yell, but his voice was muffled by the handkerchief that was rammed in his mouth.

Jack could feel that the syringe was empty, so he forced his hand down inside his pocket violently breaking the needle off and leaving it protruding from his victim's neck. The extra pain from this action and the panic of his situation caused more struggling from the lad and he flailed his arms in some desperate but futile attempt to free himself. Jack ignored these forceful lunges and just clung to him as if he were a python crushing his prey. It was only a matter of seconds before Jack felt his victim's struggles cease as the effects of the Dizampathene gradually paralysed the young man's body. He released his grip and his victim flopped face-first onto the paving blocks, unable to speak or move.

Jack casually took the man-bag from his shoulder and placed it carefully onto the ground. He seemingly now ignored his victim, who had a trickle of blood coming from a small wound on his nose from where he had hit the paving slab face first. Jack removed the rolled-up leather surgical instrument case from the bag, untied it, and neatly unfolded it onto the slab next to where the young man was lying. He pulled the balled-up handkerchief from his victim's mouth, he was now confident the Dizampathene had paralysed his vocal cords. Jack looked into his captive's eyes and with his insanity growing said. "Please call out for help if you can," tormenting his captive and only adding to his terror. Jack then turned away and placed the handkerchief in his man bag giving a small violent shudder as he did so.

Jack's demeanour had changed. He oozed a wicked unfeeling aura and was now just focused on every dark detail of his merciless undertaking. Rising to his feet he removed his long trench coat, which was encumbering him slightly. With the coat off, he folded it neatly and placed it onto one of the nearby thick gorse bushes. It was these thick, entangled bushes that were to give him the cover to undertake his terrible deeds. Jack crouched by his victim again, once again reaching into the man bag, this time removing a small pristine white square cloth, then the two long lengths of coarse string and finally a pair of long latex surgeon's gloves. He pulled the gloves onto his hands and up his hairy forearms. The hairs on his arms stood on end as if every part of his body was being stimulated by the excitement of this whole murderous experience. Now with his hands gloved, Jack had a sudden realisation of the helpless young man's presence at the scene once again. He reached down and violently took hold of his victim's hair. Gripping his curls tightly, he used them to turn over the lad's paralysed body. There was obvious terror in the young man's eyes as he now lay looking up panic-stricken at his merciless attacker. "Time for you then, lover," Jack said, as he drew a deep deliberate breath of air. He breathed out slowly and for a minute was once again gentle as he unfolded the white square cloth and laid it precisely on the ground. This break in depravity was only a short prelude and the madness was about to begin in earnest.

Jack snatched a large scalpel from the surgeon's roll. He held it up admiringly and then used it to cut away the young man's slightly soiled tee shirt and then his tight jeans. He dragged the clothing from his victim leaving him naked and exposed. Finally, he pulled off his victim's shoes and placed them together in a deliberate and exacting ritual fashion on the dirt beside the paving slab. He then replaced the large scalpel into its precise pocket of the leather roll. The recumbent body of the lad was easily manipulated by Jack and he tied both his victim's ankles together with a piece of the coarse string after forcing them violently behind each of his conquest's goose-pimpled thighs, just as he had with his first victim. Without hesitation, Jack turned his attention to the young man's paralysed hands and arms wrenching them awkwardly behind his back before binding these brutally with the other piece of coarse string and in a similar fashion to the way he had the lad's ankles "Now you are bound to please," Jack muttered to himself, his madness growing with every passing minute.

Jack had a method of killing, and he followed each step in a precise ritualistic fashion. He reached out and took the smallest scalpel from the leather roll and gently brushed each of the young man's nipples to make them pert. He expertly removed them one at a time. Then both were symmetrically and precisely placed on the crisp white cloth on the ground. Jack replaced the small scalpel in the roll and took out the second-largest surgical blade from the leather holder. He leaned over his victim's helpless body and his eyes blackened again. His personality was swinging between gentle premeditated insanity, to the acts of a deranged ferocious madman.

Jack stared coldly into his desperate captive's eyes. He snatched at his victim's hair, wrenching his head forward, so the young man could witness the savagery that he was going to inflict on his naked torso. "Watch this," Jack said quietly but deliberately and in a very disturbed manner. He drew the sharp blade down the full length of the young man's body from just below the sternum to just above the pelvic area. The cut was very deep but the blade was so sharp it was more than a minute before it sprang open, as if in a sudden realisation that the flesh was cut. The Dizampathene inhibited the blood flow but some still leeched from the gaping wound. With his victim still looking on, Jack reached in and opened the wound further and with his now trembling gloved hands pulled at the exposed intestines that protruded from it. As he did so his victim's body contorted and his pupils could be seen to dilate registering the immense pain of such a violent intrusion. He laid the ruptured, grey, bloody sausage-like intestine on the still-conscious young man's stomach and chest and with this barbaric act completed, Jack shuddered violently. His body was shaking, almost fitting with the trembling intensity of his savage actions.

Jack was in full murderous flight; this act of depravity had fuelled his lust for blood. He picked up the scalpel again and this time drove the blade ferociously into his helpless victim's neck. The weapon deeply embedded, Jack twisted it brutally. He then dragged the large cutting instrument in a jagged motion right across his still terrified victim's throat. The blade ripped through the flesh of the young man's neck, shattering cartilage and sinew and after a few seconds sprang open, leaving a huge gaping wound. The young man started choking, he was trembling violently. Jack starred wickedly at him, watching him drowning in his own blood and totally unable to breathe.

Jack's body went into a further thrilled spasm of excitement with this extra suffering of his victim. He was bursting with an almost demonic energy. Frenzied he moved the blade again, this time into the victim's groin. He slashed at the young man's genitals, removing them in several hacking motions and held them up as if they were a trophy. This display lasted just a few seconds and then he forced the bloodied genitals into his now-dead victim's open mouth.

Jack, by this time, was completely out of control; he slashed wildly at the corpse, attacking both the thighs and buttocks. He shuddered violently again. Suddenly, his head fell forwards and as if all the madness surging through him had left him for a second, he gave a huge sigh which signalled his release from this frenetic activity. Jack paused for a moment and then drew a deep breath desperate to recharge his lungs and his body with oxygen, the madness drained every ounce of strength from him. Just as he did so he heard a noise nearby that alarmed him, a voice, someone was close. He knelt motionless, frozen like a statue and with the fresh blood still staining the blade on his scalpel. He didn't dare even breathe out. But seconds later the voice was gone, and with much relief, he released the air from his lungs. He was safe.

Jack looked at his lifeless victim and studied him showing no emotion, just a calm emptiness. He wiped the blade of the large scalpel against the flesh of the mutilated corpse and replaced the half-cleaned instrument in the leather roll. Next, he pulled the smallest scalpel out again from another pouch in the roll and with exacting precision, cut four deep straight vertical lines into the left cheek of the corpse before replacing this blade also.

Jack wasn't finished yet; he reached into his man bag, this time taking out a carefully folded note, which he placed on the ground beside the mutilated corpse. Quite methodically, he took the largest scalpel from the roll. Jack shuffled his position and almost as if performing surgery, he reached into the upper part of the victim's exposed torso. Pushing past the small intestine he forced the scalpel up to an area just under the ribcage, where part of the victim's liver was exposed. In completing such an invasive action he ruptured and mutilated the internal organs of the victim further, only adding to the carnage and devastation inside the already mangled frame. With precision, he cut away a large chunky, bloody piece of dark liver, pulling it expertly away from the main part of the inside of the destroyed body. Jack squeezed the piece of liver slightly; it was still quite warm and for a moment he seemed insanely fascinated by it.

He used the large piece of liver as a paperweight, placing it onto the folded piece of paper that he had previously put beside the corpse. This operation completed he replaced the large blade in the leather roll. He wiped his heavily bloodied glove on the torso and then reached back into the man bag removing the small phial of blood he had brought with him. Jack took off the surgical glove from his left hand and placed it on the ground. Opening the phial he poured a small amount of the blood from it onto the palm of the glove. Carefully and gently and without any signs of his previous brutality, he lifted the still-bound right hand of the dead young man. He then pushed the fingers of the corpse through the blooded glove, ensuring some of the blood transferred up and under the fingernails of the victim's hand.

His murderous work here was almost done. Jack stood up and picked up the surgical glove and the half-empty phial of blood He then removed his other glove and placed all the items in the man-bag. Kneeling once again, he rolled up the leather surgeon's case and tied it neatly before placing that too into his bag. He paused for a minute checking to make sure the scene was as he wanted it. Jack noticed the empty syringe had fallen from inside his coat pocket during the violence of the attack and he bent down to pick it up and then packed that away also. He gave a self-satisfying smile and stood up again. One more check to be sure everything was as he wanted it and then he prepared himself to leave the scene of carnage.

Jack lifted his coat from the nearby bushy branch, unfolded it and put it on. Emerging from the hideaway he checked and carefully surveyed his surroundings. No one was close by. He walked slowly away and rejoined the footpath and this time followed it up onto the main seafront road. As he got to the top of the path he paused for a moment looking back and a dark demonic smile painted across his face. Under his breath and with a manic depraved tone, he whispered the words. "*Death becomes you,*", and he set off back towards the security of Compton Street.

CHAPTER EIGHT

Suddenly all hell broke loose on the C.I.D. floor. A young uniformed constable shouted to two detectives who stood in the corridor. "Where is the detective chief inspector?" His voice was vibrating with urgency.

"In the skipper's office, I think," one of the detectives said. "He is just going home it has been a very long day." The constable knocked frantically at the door to the sergeant's office. Sergeant Carter opened the door, and the young constable almost threw himself into the room.

"There's been another killing, sir," the young constable blurted out. "Dukes Mound, Dukes Mound," he said. "The body has just been found."

"Right let's go, John," Martin said. "No going home for us now. Right, constable, can you go to the incident room straight away, tell the officers there what has happened and tell them their duty is being extended."

"Yes, sir, of course," the constable replied having now got his breath back.

"And tell them they need to stay at 'the nick' until we get back. They can go to the bar and grab a bite to eat; they have earned it, and it could be a long Saturday night yet." With that, the two detectives hurried away along the corridor and down the stairs.

Minutes later the pair arrived at the scene; it was now a quarter past six in the early evening and the east end of Dukes Mound was already a frenetic hive of activity. Several uniformed officers were cordoning the area off and two scenes of crime officers were donning forensic suits. "Who's the informant?" Martin asked one of the uniformed constables who stood nearby.

"It was called in anonymously, on the nines," the P.C. replied. "From a seafront call box, I think, sir."

"Oh that's bloody great, all we need," Martin said. "Right, in that case, John, tell the communications room I want that call traced and get every phone box local to this part of the seafront sealed. Make sure there is a uniformed officer at each of them to stop them from being used until we can establish which phone box the informant called in from. When the phone box used for the informant's call has been identified, get it examined thoroughly by S.O.C.O., John. The informant still could be our killer. Right, let's have a look and see what we have got this time."

More crime scene officers and supporting units had arrived at the incident. The police had locked the scene down to protect the integrity of any evidence that might be found there. "Phone boxes are secured, sir. I have got constables going to each one," Carter said as he and Martin went into the newly erected incident tent. Once inside they saw Mary Marshall, the pathologist, who had been called just as she was going home and had been able to get to the scene quickly. "We have got to stop meeting like this, Mary," Carter jibed.

"Have you any first impressions, Mary?" Martin said.

"Well," said Marshall. "For now it looks like the same M.O. as the other body, Tim. The victim is a young man and has been mutilated in a similar pattern to one at the railway station and there are lines carved in the face again."

"Oh shit, you know what that means!" Martin

breathed out a huge sigh.

"Yes, Tim, at the moment it looks like it's the same killer. The wounds are the same, inflicted the same way and the genitals are rammed in the mouth again. There appears also to be blood under the fingernails of the victim's right hand, but it's too early at this time to know whose it is, and whether it is the victim's or potentially any attackers," she added. "Oh and look," she went on. "The lines carved in the face." She pointed to them. "It seems this time there are only four and what is that on the far side of the corpse? Look just under the torso to the left, it appears to be a piece of human liver if I'm not mistaken, with a folded piece of paper beneath it!"

"Yes, it looks as if it is another note, sir," Carter said.

"Okay," Martin said. "Let's get suited and gloved up and we can examine the body more closely." The chief inspector then proceeded to give out a few precise instructions to the officers gathered nearby. Then he and his sergeant went back into the now completely assembled incident tent. There were crime scene officers and Marshall already inside.

Martin made small talk with Marshall for a minute. "Our victim has some I.D. on him," Carter interjected. "There is a driving licence in his wallet in the name of Mr. Simon Halls. According to his date of birth on the licence he's aged twenty-two. And there is a wad of business cards offering male-to-male massage services. There is also over two hundred pounds in cash. Another young male prostitute and we certainly can rule out robbery," Carter added.

"This is no attempted robbery, John, as you say; no, sadly this killer is murdering for kicks! Okay, so we need the victim's identity confirmed and let's have a look at this note," Martin said. Marshall removed the piece of coagulated liver pinning the note to the ground and then carefully bagged it. She then unfolded the blood-stained note found resting underneath it and just under the mangled torso. She was as interested as the two police officers to see what it said this time. "It's another verse," she sighed.

"Well read it out, but quietly please," Martin said as he leant down looking at the bound, mutilated corpse. "This is a fresh one Mary? He has not been dead long."

"No, no," Marshall said. "Not long, a couple of hours, maybe more."

"Okay read the note then," Martin said.

"Phew," Marshall puffed out her cheeks this time.

> "My second victim, death does taint,
>
> Be him a sinner and not a saint,
>
> Crowded streets for blame does cause,
>
> The murdering of your worthless whores."

"Bloody hell Mary, what on earth do you make of that?" Carter asked enquiringly.

"Well," Marshall replied. "There are references to crowded cities, isn't that what was blamed for 'Jack the Ripper' never getting caught," she said.

"Blimey," Carter said. "You know your 'Ripper' history, Mary."

"Yes, yes, the case always fascinated me," the pathologist replied, still staring at the note in her gloved hand.

"Well, whatever," Martin said. He certainly was in

no mood for a 'Ripper' history lesson.

"Let's leave the note for now; I think it's a distraction we don't need," Martin retorted curtly. The chief inspector found the notes of these recent murders not only upsetting, but he also despised the thought anyone could make taunts after murdering another human being in such a brutal fashion.

He was almost dismissive of their content. Marshall, however, thought the quatrain notes more significant. She spoke up, "With another 'Jack the Ripper' like reference I feel I am now sure this murderer is inventing himself as a copycat 'Ripper?' she said.

"I bloody hope not, Mary, that's all we need," Martin replied. However, he knew she was more than certainly right in her evaluation; he also knew that copycat killers were always likely to follow the pattern of their idols and keep killing until either caught or killed themselves. "That's all we bloody need!" he repeated.

Back at the John Street police station, Martin and Carter had the detectives in an emergency early evening briefing. "I'm sorry it's been a long day for all of us," Martin said. "But I need to sort out this mess thus far, so we will carry on working until twenty-three hundred hours." A huge sigh of discontentment went round the room. "Settle down. Come on, people. Okay, these are the facts to date for you," Martin said blowing air from his cheeks. "There has been, as you know, another killing which was reported anonymously on the nines at seventeen fifty today. Our victim has been confirmed as Mr Simon Halls; he was aged twenty-two and was also a confirmed male prostitute like our first victim. I have already detailed uniformed officers to track down any next of kin of the latest victim. The phone box that was used to report the incident has been traced and this is being subjected to close forensic analysis. On the second whiteboard in the briefing room, there are pictures of both the two victims. Both were mutilated and beyond recognition of having once been healthy young men. Same M.O., so we are linking them." There was a quiet rumble of voices that went around the briefing room. Everyone knew the significance of multiple killings by one murderer.

"And there is another note!" Sergeant Carter said with a sarcastic desperation.

"Yes, yes," Martin said. "There is a copy of it on the board; you had better all read it just in case it sheds any light on the case at some time. There were no prints on it and the handwriting is the same as was on the first note. The paper used is a generic plain white sheet, so no clues from that other than the verse itself."

"Which still smacks of bloody lunatic to me," Sergeant Carter interjected.

"Yes I agree, but a very dangerous one," Martin added. "Whilst we are on the subject of the poems, our handwriting expert believes, from the first note, that our killer is left-handed. Worth putting in your pocket notebooks," Martin said. Another ripple went around the room.

"Right settle down," Sergeant Carter said.

"Also, I have just had the report back on the blood under the fingernails of our first victim," Martin said taking the lead again. "It is that of a Mr. George Williams; he is aged sixty-seven and we have a home address for him in Patcham. At the moment he is our number one suspect. I want D.C. Smith and D.C. Thomas on this, away you go, you two. I want to know where Williams has been, his work, his movements and what he has had for breakfast. Bring him in to help us with our enquiries but don't arrest him unless you have to, we don't have enough evidence yet, and if he is our killer, I don't want to give him any indication that we know his blood is at the scene. Let us know when you get back with him, I want to interview him myself, Becky."

The two officers, Martin had tasked, left the briefing room. "Okay the rest of you, it's carry on from where you were time." Martin raised his eyes to D.C. Andrew and D.C. Fuller. "Any luck tracing the Dizampathene, you two?"

"Well, there have been no recent burglaries at any pharmacies, sir, and it's a pretty specialised drug. The manufacturers have given us a short list of places they supply, but the only local ones seem to be two small pharmacies and our own Royal Sussex County Hospital."

"Okay," Martin replied. "You two get yourselves to those establishments and see if they can tell if they have any Dizampathene missing and let me know anything as soon as you know."

It was only a matter of half an hour or so and D.C. Thomas and D.C. Smith returned to the John Street station with the very bemused Mr. Williams. "He wasn't keen to come in, sir, but he is in interview room two."

"I don't suppose he was," Martin said.

"Okay, thanks, you two. See if you can get out and ask around about our second victim, and find out if he worked at Dukes Mound regularly and if anyone knows him well. Oh, and find out if he and Clarke are linked in any way other than selling themselves. Also, tell all the young prostitutes to take extra care. Let them know there have been two killings that are possibly linked, but be subtle, we don't want to cause panic. Yes and go to Maggie, to Maggie Anne's place up by the station, that old tart knows everyone and everything that's going on in the city and she owes us," Martin went on.

Maggie Anne was well known to the police in Brighton. She sat in the window of her upstairs flat which was situated near the railway station in Dacre Road and often stuck a finger or two up at the passing police patrol cars. She was nearly sixty-five and had worked the streets of Brighton as a prostitute for many years. Her activities were largely turned a blind eye to by the local coppers; she was a good informant and harmless. The two detectives knocked at the front door of the flat.

"Piss off," a woman's voice was heard to shout through the door. "Whoever you are, it's too late in the day, you can 'piss off'," she was heard to say again.

"Now that's not very friendly, Maggie," Detective Thomas replied. "It's the police; can we have a word?"

"Oh for fucks sake," the woman said. "I'm not decent, wait a bloody minute." After a couple of minutes, a pair of high-heeled shoes could be heard clattering along the hallway of the first-floor flat. The door opened, still on its chain. "You got I.D.?" the woman said.

"Of course," the young female detective replied, and both she and D.C. Smith showed her their warrant cards, both of which the ageing woman scarcely glanced at. As she took the chain off and opened the door she came into full view of the two detectives. She was wearing a short black dressing gown which had a fluffy pink collar and black high-heeled mule-type shoes. Her make-up was heavy and she had a lit cigarette hanging from her bottom lip and her breath smelt strongly of gin. "Who has bloody died then?" she said, as she beckoned the two detectives into the well-decorated and immaculately clean flat.

"Why would you think anyone's died, Maggie?" Dave Smith said with a small grin.

"Only time you lot come and fucking see me," she replied tartly. "Sit down," she said to the two detective constables. "I can't make you tea. I have got a friend due in fifteen minutes and he'd have a fucking fit if he finds you two in here!"

"Okay, Maggie, I'll make it brief," D.C. Thomas said. "We have had two young male prostitutes brutally killed over the last few days and both, we believe at this time, were killed by the same person. The first was a lad who we now know was working the railway station and was killed in the yard behind it."

"Oh bloody hell, someone told me the station was swarming with police but we all thought it was another fucking I.R.A. bomb scare. You kept that quiet," the old woman added. "I know there are a few young lads that trick at that railway station; where was the other one killed?"

"Dukes Mound, Maggie," the detective replied.

"Oh well, that's no surprise, that's a place that is, all them bushes and what goes on down there, would make your bleeding hair curl it would."

"Yes, we know that only too well, Maggie," Dave Smith said with a wry smile again.

"I bet you bloody do, love," the prostitute replied and laughed.

"So, you haven't heard anything, Maggie?"

Detective Thomas asked.

"No, love," the old woman said to the female detective, "but I'll ask around for you and see what I can find out."

"Thanks, Maggie, but please be discreet."

"Okay, love, yes, yes, I'll do that, give me a couple of days and pop back. So sad when people die so young; most of these lads selling themselves have had a tough enough start as it is. It's a funny old life sometimes. Now, darlings, as much as I enjoy your company, I'm afraid I'm going to have to ask the pair of you to 'piss off' as I already told you, I have a friend coming around and I have got to get my outfit on."

As they left and walked back to the waiting car the young female detective turned to Dave Smith and said, "What outfit do you think she meant?"

"I think I'd rather die in ignorance!" he replied. "Let's get back to 'the nick'."

CHAPTER NINE

Sergeant Carter and Martin were now in interview room two. It was a modern tape-recorded interview suite and the officers identified themselves and then identified Mr Williams to the tape machine. "You are not currently under arrest, Mr Williams, but I am going to caution you," the detective chief inspector said, and he relayed the official caution to Mr. Williams. "Oh, and you can have a solicitor if you want one?" Martin said.

"I don't need a bloody solicitor," Williams replied. "I haven't done anything."

Martin relayed to Williams the facts and the detained man was clearly shocked to find his blood had been found under the fingernails of a young murder victim at the city railway station. "I've never been to that yard, truly, truly I haven't." His voice was desperate.

"Okay, where were you between three-thirty and five-thirty on Wednesday the fifteenth?" Martin asked.

"I was in the hospital," Williams replied, "in the local Brighton Hospital and unconscious. I was having a torn meniscus repaired in my knee." Both the detectives just looked at each other. "You can check. Please, check," Williams added. His voice was fraught but relieved.

"We will, Mr. Williams. Okay, check that will you please, John? Right; interview suspended," Martin said and recorded the time of the interview suspension on the tape. His police radar told him this was a man telling the truth, and he was now looking at Mr.

Williams in a completely different light.

"I think we could both do with a coffee, Mr. Williams," he said. "John, get three coffees on your way back will you please?"

It was not long before Sergeant Carter returned to the interview room; the two men, Martin and Mr. Williams were chatting in a more relaxed fashion. "His story checks out, sir," Carter said as he came back into the room and put down a small tray with the vending machine hot drinks. "He went down for surgery at fourteen-fifty and did not come off the recovery ward until seventeen-fifty. He was discharged from the hospital at twenty-one hundred hours; the hospital they have verified all the facts."

"Oh, thank God for that," Williams said, his hand still shaking as he sipped his coffee.

"Okay, well Mr. Williams you are free to go for now but we will have to investigate further the matter of how your blood was found at the crime scene. It may be we will need to talk to you again. We would please ask you to keep what we have told you to yourself. This is an awkward enough investigation as it is."

A much relieved Mr. Williams was released, and Martin and Carter returned to the C.I.D. suite and found all the detective constables were back at the John Street police station. Martin addressed them, "Let's have one last meeting in the incident room; it will be twenty- three hundred hours soon, we all need to get home and get some rest."

All the detective constables had completed their allotted tasks and had returned to the John Street police station for the daily debrief. None had been able to speak directly to Martin yet as he had been tied up interviewing Mr. Williams. That done, Martin was keen to find out what, if anything, his team had discovered. He went into the incident room where everyone was now gathered. "Okay, so who wants to start and tell me some bloody good news please, people," Martin said.

D.C. Hopkins spoke up. "Well, sir, magnificent Maggie Anne" – the detective constable said sarcastically, to a ripple of muted giggles and laughter – "Is asking around, governor; she hasn't heard anything to date. After I dropped Becky back at 'the nick' both D.C. Thompson and I went around a few of the other local prostitutes and their favoured pubs and bars asking discretely about Clarke, but it seems he was very much a loner. The only thing everyone said was that he liked cocaine, unsurprisingly. We did as you had said and told all the young prostitutes we saw to take extra care on the streets and to tell all their friends. We told them there had been two killings that were possibly linked and that they all should be more vigilant."

"Okay, yes well done."

"They were all very blasé' about the warning; none seemed particularly interested, governor."

"Well," Martin said. "It's as much as we can do for now. I don't want to be too alarmist but at least hopefully the word will spread and they will take a bit more care. I'm going to speak to Superintendent Flowers in the morning and take his advice on whether we should do a press release as there have been two murders, but we will cross that bridge tomorrow. Right," Martin went on, "and what about the hospital and pharmacies; how did you two get on with those, any joy?" Martin lifted his eyes to D.C.'s Fuller and Andrews.

"Neither of the pharmacies had kept any stock of Dizampathene for ages. The Royal Sussex County Hospital keep a limited amount of Dizampathene all the time but they had no one to check their stocks in the controlled drug cabinets at this time of night, sir. They have stated it will be done first thing tomorrow and they'll get back to us with the results. We also asked around as to who might have access to the controlled drug cabinets as a matter of routine and got some names. We have checked a couple, but need to follow up with several more tomorrow."

"Okay," Martin said. "Have we any details on our second victim's family yet, Becky?"

"The uniform guys have just got back to me, sir. He had only one relative, his father who lives in Manchester. I have got the local boys there to go and break the sad news to him. I understand from them that his father is in a home and is suffering from Alzheimer's disease so it could be a dead end. The other thing I found out is Clarke, as the boys said, was a loner. He has a long-term history of drug abuse and several minor convictions for theft, a known male prostitute, that's about it I'm afraid."

"Okay, so we are just running up blind alleys at the moment," Martin said. "Let's just hope Marshall and S.O.C.O. can come up with something, we need that bloody informant! Alright then, night everyone, thanks for today. I'm changing all your duties. I want everyone back here at seven in the morning." Turning to his sergeant Martin said, "Right that's us, John. I told you I had a bad feeling about this one, my old friend, let's go home. I'm knackered."

The next morning Martin was in work as usual at six

o'clock sharp. He had received an email from Marshall who had worked into the night on completing the full second autopsy and she had asked him to meet her in the morning at the morgue. Scenes of crime officers had also found some partial fingerprints inside the phone box that had been used by the informant who had rang the station and these were going to be followed up later that day in the hope of identifying them further. Martin had been at work for nearly half an hour and as he sipped at his hot coffee preparing his morning briefing, D.C. Tony Hopkins and two of the other detective constables suddenly came rushing into his office.

"Have you seen the papers, sir? Have you seen them?" Hopkins was panicked. "Look at that, sir, look at that."

Martin picked up the Sunday newspaper, the headlines read:

"Does Brighton have a Serial Killer? Read our exclusive story direct from the man who found a body at Dukes Mound."

The article was detailed and made devastating reading for the senior detective. Journalists claimed to have pictures of the victim. They had listed the injuries on the body in graphic detail and of their own volition had linked this latest murder with the one at the Brighton railway station. Their report stated that their informant had gone to the paper fearing what accusations the police might make against him. The article had even described the killer as, "The Brighton Ripper".

"This is all we fucking need," Martin said, his voice raised a notch to emphasise his total despair. "He's sold his bloody story, we are going to have every want to be 'Ripper' nut calling us to confess and it's going to cause panic in the whole community. We have to get this under control. We must trace this informant. Get onto the paper, Becky, and find out who the hell he is. They cannot withhold that information and we need it!" The detective chief inspector's phone rang. "Get that will you please?" Martin said. Sergeant Carter and all the other detectives had arrived for duty by this point and had heard the commotion in their boss's office.

Carter picked up the phone. "It's the superintendent, sir," he said. "He's seen the papers and has come in early; he wants to see you in his office 'now'!"

"Get everyone on their duties, John," Martin relayed to his sergeant. "I will go and see the super. Don't let anyone leave 'the nick' yet. Before anyone goes out I want us all to have a meeting in the incident room. I want to make certain everyone keeps their cool. Once they leave 'the nick' there is every chance they'll get harassed by reporters. This bloody newspaper article has changed the dynamics of the case. We are going to need a slight change of tack and I want all involved on their 'A' game. Can you also try and see when Marshall is back in at the morgue? She messaged me late last night. I'm hoping she has some news. Can you sort that?"

"Yes governor, of course. Get going," Carter said. "The super did not sound in the frame of mind to be kept waiting! We've already had two blokes losing their balls this week and that is quite enough!" Carter's joke at least took a little tension out of the air.

Martin raised his eyebrows. "You are not wrong, John," he replied and he puffed out his cheeks. "Wish me luck," he said and he went along the corridor and up the stairs in the direction of the superintendent's office.

Superintendent Flowers was waiting in his office as the detective chief inspector knocked at the door. The two men had had their differences in the past and Flowers, who had been fast-tracked to promotion, was considered by Martin to be a yes-man. He thought the senior officer had climbed the service ladder because of his connections within the job. This was going to be a strained meeting. "What the hell is going on, Tim?" Flowers said. "I don't appreciate having to come in at this time of the morning because my senior officers cannot keep a lid on the press."

"With all due respect, sir, as far as the press are concerned, I locked down the first killing. And whoever found the second body went straight to the journalists after reporting it to us and then obviously sold them the story."

"Okay. So I need you to find out who he or she bloody is! We need to stop this from escalating any further. Do we have any leads?" Flowers asked.

"I only found out myself half an hour ago, sir. The press has stated the informant was a man, but I need to verify that. I have got detectives working on the press, if they know who the informant is we will find out. He still could be our killer."

"I know that, chief inspector!" Flowers retorted his voice quivered with frustration. "And what other leads do we have?"

"We have some D.N.A. evidence and ongoing enquiries at the hospital." Martin started to show his own frustrations. "But I am not going to catch anyone standing up here with you arguing the toss, sir. I do not control the press and I cannot be held responsible for any headlines or stories that they choose to put into print! I'm as horrified as you are it is certainly not helping my investigations or the team's morale," he added. Martin's voice was raised; he was not going to be walked on, especially by Flowers.

The superintendent's attitude had calmed; he had been enraged by the story in the newspaper, mainly because of the backlash it would have on him and on the political tightrope he walked as a very senior police officer. The senior officer already had reporters starting to gather in small numbers outside the front of the John Street police station, something that always meant stressful days were ahead. Flowers, however, knew Martin was a very good detective and despite their differences, he knew he would not deliberately bring the job into disrepute, or let the press all over a case. Martin was straight, honest and direct; he also was not influenced, no matter what anyone else thought, by any prejudice of either gender or race. Flowers knew this first hand; he was in a minority when he had at first joined the job because he was of black African origin. As a young constable, Martin had been his sergeant. During this time – on several occasions – he had been out on the streets with Martin and had suffered racist abuse from aggressive prisoners and even sometimes the general public. Martin had always taken the toughest approach to this. Martin had the senior officer's admiration for his ability as a detective, even though Flowers now outranked him.

We need an arrest for this one, Tim, and we need it quickly for all our sakes." Flowers' said.

"Then, sir, please, just let me go and get on with

my job, I want this bastard as badly as you do, press or no press," Martin said.

The superintendent raised his eyebrows. "Okay, Tim, right," he sighed. "I'm going to set up a press conference. I will give them all the usual spiel; I'll tell them we have the situation under control there will be more officers on the beat and that we are working night and day etc, etc. Hopefully, this will buy you some more time. I'll also get a dedicated incident hotline organised for the public to call in with information relating to the case."

"That will be way too much work for my team, sir," Martin said.

"Don't worry, I'll use some communication room and Whisky Victor C.C.T.V. officers to man the phones, to free up your men, Tim, and we will get a direct dial number for the public asking for information about these murders. It will open the floodgates but we need to be completely transparent on this one. I will stress to those involved, to filter the calls as much as practicable and try not to load you up too much more with what is called in. You never know 'Joe public' may just have that gem of information we need and it will placate the press and buy us some time."

Martin saw a more human side to his boss as the superintendent sighed and said, "Get this bastard soon, Tim, or we will both be back knocking on doors!" Martin turned to go out of the office. As he walked away to go out of the room he heard his senior officer pick up the phone. "This is Superintendent Flowers. I want a press conference at midday" he said. "Get it sorted."

Martin knew a press conference was like going into the lion's den and as he shut his senior officer's door,

Martin whispered. "Rather you than me sir, yes rather you than me."

After visiting the communications room and the toilet, the detective chief inspector got back to the major incident briefing room.

"How was it, sir?" Carter enquired cautiously.

"Flowers, oh he was okay, better than expected. Perhaps he's human after all," Martin laughed. "He's doing a press conference, all the usual information. We are working towards an arrest, cooperation of the public and press is needed, as well as extra public awareness in their meeting strangers, and there will be additional uniformed officers on the streets. You know the brief. In truth I don't think it's only the press that worries him, it's the politics of it all and those he has to answer to in the upper circle. He was fair and it's not just my balls on the block with this one, is it? Our senior officer's reputation rides on this as much as ours. Call the troops in, John, will you? Let's see where we are and who has got what."

The incident room was buzzing; the press story had caught everyone by surprise and there was more than just an air of tension circulating. More officers had been drafted in on the case and Sergeant Carter had given them a refresher up-to-date briefing. Everyone in the room knew that the pressure to catch this particular killer was heightened. In fairness, the story was a journalist's dream; but it was also a nightmare for the police.

"Okay, people," Martin said. "So we all know the score now with the newspaper story. Nothing has changed for us. We still want this bastard caught; we just need to act quickly and no one, I repeat, no one, tells the press anything without my say-so.

Superintendent Flowers" – a little jeer was heard to ripple through the room. Flowers was not any of the detective's favourite senior officer – "Superintendent Flowers," Martin continued, "has been fair with this one; he is calling a bloody press conference and giving us extra officers. I don't know about you, but I wouldn't swap places with him right now. On the downside, he's setting up a public hotline for information, so we will soon be inundated with intelligence to check. It's going to get very busy, people. I'm leaving it to you as individuals to trust your judgement on any information you are passed. We all know what constitutes a good lead, so let's be thorough but astute. So, before the ensuing madness starts," Martin sighed. "We need this drug traced as I said before. So it's back to the hospital. We need to know urgently if they have discovered that any drugs are missing. Becky, how is it going with the paper? We need the details of that informant. He is the best lead we have at the moment."

"I'm on it," the female detective constable replied. "I am expecting a call-back today but they are giving me the run-around."

"Okay, so find out the name of the reporter who wrote the story. Let's go straight to him or her," Martin said, his voice expressing urgency. "That's your priority job, Becky. Let me know when you find out as soon as possible. We have had no leads at all from the C.C.T.V. at the railway station and no luck with Maggie Anne, our reliable informant thus far. I want the fingerprint reports chased from the phone box and every person identified from them. These persons will all also then need to be traced and interviewed. Anyone not working on these leads, I want out talking to the gay community, bars, pubs you know the score. Someone out there knows something we need to know!"

Sergeant Carter took a step forward. "In addition," he added. "From this point on we want everyone to collate all their information to date on these four whiteboards I have prepared here." He pointed at a neat row of newly mounted large whiteboards at the side of the room. "We are going to use these to share information with the team," Carter said. "Hot info is to be written in red and everything else in black."

Martin took the lead again. "One more thing," he said. "And this is important. No one goes out without telling the communications room where they are going; this killer is dangerous. Come on, people, we need to get this case nailed!" The detective chief inspector's voice was emphatic.

CHAPTER TEN

The following morning the detectives all soon gathered and sat in their usual early morning briefing positions as Martin brought them up to date with the events thus far. "Right okay," he said. The detective chief inspector then turned his eyes to D.C. Dave Smith. "Dave," Martin said to the experienced detective constable. "From this point on, you are the collations officer; check all the information anyone puts on the boards and keep a rolling record of the investigation for myself and Superintendent Flowers. Give us a copy of it every night before you go off duty. Sorry, I know it's not a glamorous job, Dave," he added. "But you are so good with detail."

"It's his O.C.D., sir," Becky retorted. A little ripple of laughter went around the room. Martin ignored the comment, barely hearing it as he was so consumed by the details of the case.

"It's still twelve-hour shifts everyone, we will all meet up back here at eighteen- hundred hours when we will have a catch-up debrief on the work of the day. Right, that's it, I want to know what they say at the hospital about any missing drugs as soon as possible Hopkins, message me." The detectives started leaving the room. There was tension in the air, but this was a good team, they worked hard and played hard.

"Marshall said can we go up to the morgue when you are free from the briefing, governor," Carter said.

"Oh yes, I know," Martin replied. "I expect she is wondering where we have bloody got to," he added. "Okay, John let's go and let's hope she has some good news this time. I'm about done with nasty surprises. I just need a quick piss and we will go." With that, the phone in the detective chief inspector's office rang.

"I'll get that, sir," Carter said. "You go and have a pee. Detective Chief Inspector Martin's office," the sergeant said as he lifted the phone, hoping it was good news. "Yes, right, I will tell him. He is not going to like it, though," the sergeant sighed.

Martin returned from the restroom. "You look stressed, John," he said. "Oh fuck, what on earth now?"

"Councillor Morgan is in reception, governor. He's seen the papers and wants to speak to you. He's adamant."

Martin and the councillor were old foes and had crossed swords many times before. Councillor Morgan hated the police without exception and also thought that officers yielded too many unaccountable powers. Morgan was homosexual and in his personal opinion, considered many police officers to be homophobic. He was a serious adversary for Martin holding as he did, a senior position in the local community. His personal hatred for the police had developed from being arrested years before when he was a young man and subsequently being prosecuted for a gross indecency offence with another man in a public toilet.

"Go to the front office to tell him I have left 'the nick'," Martin said to his sergeant. "I'm not in the mood this morning to see Councillor Morgan; besides, Marshall may have something I can placate the councillor with," Martin said.

"I fucking doubt that!" Carter replied. "Okay, on your head it will be then, governor, I'll tell the front office to tell him you are out. I'm sure he will entertain himself for a short while, talking to the reporters I saw gathering earlier outside the front of 'the nick'," he added and laughed.

Marshall and the two detectives were standing in the main holding area of the morgue. The pathologist was clutching a large shiny blue folder, and in front of her were both victims' bodies from the two murders; both were covered on trolleys with just their bare feet exposed.

"Well," Marshall said. "It is the same killer, as I told you in the report I sent over. It's the same method of operation. This latest victim was tied up in the same way as the first, with no specialist knots or uncommon types of string having been used. The killer then started by removing the nipples after drugging the victim and moved on from there. Wounds were identical to our first victim in that they were cut with the same surgical type of instruments.

Victim two also had had his stomach removed and laid on to his chest, his throat was cut and his genitals were severed and forced into his mouth. One difference in this latest victim was that a large part of his liver had been removed, for reasons unknown, and was placed by the killer at the side of the torso. This could have been because our killer had more time or because he was reinforcing the link to the original 'Jack the Ripper' historical murders, where the victim's organs were often removed.

In addition, our victim this time had four, not five straight lines, cut deeply into his left cheek, after he had expired. No signs of sexual contact and no semen on this one. Although there were some extra wounds in addition to the removal of part of the liver and these were made from violent slashes, this time to the thighs and buttocks of this victim. Once again there was blood under the fingernails of the right hand of the corpse, which does not match the victim's. But I got your message about the last suspect, Tim, and this blood is different again. The team have done a D.N.A. trace and the results are back. This blood belongs to a twenty-seven-year-old man. He is known to the police, hence our ease in tracing his identity on the database. All his details are in the file I sent over," Marshall said as she breathed deeply. "I don't think this is your killer's blood, Tim, especially after what happened last time. I think this killer is too clever to leave his identity at the scene. If you want my opinion, I think he is playing with you with the blood and the notes," Marshall added.

"I know," said Martin. "But we have to check. Complacency and assumptions in this job equals fuck-ups."

"Checking, however, wastes our time and buys our killer more breathing space," his sergeant said, his voice expressing a considered exasperation.

"So," Marshall said. "The reason I asked to see you is" – she paused for a moment – "If this latest blood turns out to not be your killer's, and not either of your victims, you have to just ask where the killer is getting this extra blood from, do you not!"

She knew that Martin had realised this already but just sought to reinforce the point. Martin smiled at the pathologist; he knew Marshall was thinking that this piece of evidence perhaps could be the killer's Achilles Heel and so did he. Finally, perhaps there was just a glimmer of something he could get his teeth into. Both Marshall and Martin knew the killer had some knowledge of the human body and was using surgical equipment to inflict the awful wounds. If the Dizampathene had been taken from the local hospital then their best lead was most likely a killer who worked there. Martin's mind was processing all these thoughts. Turning to Carter he said. "Let's get back to 'the factory' and see if we can eliminate this young man in the file from our enquiries. That way, John, we either catch our killer or have something to work on; the blood must be the common denominator," he said. "It just must be."

"Thanks, Mary," the two men said. Marshall felt a little hint of optimism, in this awful case, for the first time. Her forensic detection skills she hoped were paying off. Just like her police counterparts, although appalled by murders of this nature, they stimulated her brain and were the reason she loved her work.

"Good luck, you two," she replied, and the two detectives left. At least for now, they had something to work on. Both Martin and Carter had left the morgue thinking the same thing:

Our killer could be a doctor!

When Martin and Carter got back to the John Street police station, they parked in the backyard as usual. Carter turned off the engine of the silver-grey unmarked C.I.D. car and the two men sat in silence for a brief moment; both were mentally exhausted as it had been full on for them for several days now. They also had relaxed a little; they were at least getting some leads and both were feeling more optimistic. "I wonder if Morgan is still here governor?" Carter said breaking the silence.

"Oh shit, I'd forgotten about him with everything

else," Martin said. "Well, you go and track down the young man Marshall identified from the blood, John, and let me know how it goes. Don't waste our time bringing him back to 'the nick' if you can establish he is not the killer. We need these leads shut down as soon as possible," he added. "Right, well I'll go and face the music with Morgan. Let's hope he's got pissed off and left!"

The two men climbed the back stairs of the station which led from the lower entrance behind it and up to the ground floor at the front of it. Through the front office reception glass, they could see the waiting area seats and all were empty.

"You could be in luck, sir," Carter said with a smile. "There is no one waiting there!" At that moment a young uniformed constable came hurriedly down the stairs from the C.I.D. area of the first floor.

"Oh, thank God you're back, sir. Councillor Morgan's in your office. The front desk sergeant told me to put him in there because he was causing such a dreadful scene in reception and he is having enough problems keeping the press reporters out of there as it was. I have just given the councillor a coffee," the constable added. "He is spitting feathers, sir."

"About time," Morgan said as the detective chief inspector went into the office.

"Hello, councillor," Martin replied. "Yes, I am a bit busy at the moment; sorry if I have kept you waiting. What can I do for you?"

"Well," the councillor said sharply. "I have read this distressing, sickening newspaper article," he said holding a copy of the newspaper aloft for Martin to see. "And after speaking to several reporters, I have come directly to you to express my shock and concern and to see what measures you are putting in place to protect the ordinary law-abiding citizens of this city. I am the voice of the gay community, and it looks as if a heinous killer is targeting that community. I want to be sure you are treating this with all the seriousness it deserves."

Martin knew Morgan was implying that because the victims had been gay men, he and his team might not be working so hard to catch the perpetrator. Martin also knew that although Morgan was too clever to say so openly, he thought the senior policeman was homophobic and disliked gay people of all types. He was wrong on both counts.

"Councillor, I can assure you the sexual preference or gender of any murder victim is not a consideration. The need to catch any criminal under any circumstance is not subject to this, gender or race," he added. "And I find your implications an insult," Martin said.

Morgan got to his feet. What he lacked in height and stature he made up for in his deliverance of cutting remarks. "Well," he said. "Let's hope you are spending as much time on this, as harassing men in public toilets." Morgan's voice flared with emotion. "I'll be riding your coat-tails on this one, Martin. Mess up and I'll have you drummed out the force." With his venom unleashed the councillor went out of the office and slammed the door closed.

"Fucking knob," Martin muttered quietly to himself. He stood for a moment reeling but composing himself before coming out of his office and setting off in the direction of the incident room.

"Ah, sir," Detective Constable Thomas said as she saw Martin in the corridor. "I have managed to get the name of the journalist who wrote the story on the Dukes Mound murder," she said. "He is Mr. Adrian

Freeborn, a freelance reporter; he has been with the paper for a couple of years, but this is his first major story. He lives in Valley Drive at Withdean. I'm just going to see him. Do you want to tag along with me, sir?" She could see from Martin's face that he was very uptight and stressed.

"Thanks, Becky, yes I will. I could do to get some fresh air to be honest," he said. "We need this reporter to come through with some information. Did the newspaper have a name for the informant?"

"No, sir, they were very cagey about the whole affair; but they did imply that Freeborn may have more information, so I'm pinning my hopes on him at the moment, sir."

As they walked along the corridor the detective constable continued, "I have not spoken to Freeborn yet, his wife answered the home phone number I was given for him and said he had popped out for a minute. She asked me what it was about and I just said we need to speak to him about an article he wrote recently. She did not seem surprised to hear from us, the paper had probably said we would be in contact. I had just come off the phone to Freeborn's wife when I saw you, sir."

"So is Freeborn actually at home do we know?" Martin asked.

"Yes, sir, his wife told me her husband would be back in about fifteen minutes at the most, so he should be in now."

The two officers went up the long path of the well-kept home in the Valley-Drive area of Withdean. Martin rapped a large brass knocker on the substantial dark oak, front door. After a minute or so the front door opened and a tall, lanky man stood just inside the doorway. He looked at the two police officers apprehensively as they both introduced themselves and showed him their identification. "Come in," he said. All three went through into the lounge of the property. It was a well-decorated and furnished house and immaculately kept. "Please sit down. I'm Adrian Freeborn," the man said. "How can I help?"

Martin took the lead role immediately. "We are investigating a murder in the Dukes Mound area of the city. We understand from your head office, that you met a male person, who claims to be the person who discovered the body at this crime scene. I must point out to you, Mr. Freeborn that this is a very serious matter and we need all the information you have about this man."

"Am I under arrest?" Freeborn said pensively, his voice quivering with fear.

"No, not at this time," Martin said. "But we need your full cooperation. We will be noting your replies so please speak clearly and be as concise as you can."

Freeborn was nervous; the detective chief inspector watched his witness wriggle uncomfortably in his chair. "I knew you would come and see me," he said. "I said to Jane. Sorry, Jane is my wife, but I could not turn down this story, it is such a big break for me. It made the front page you know."

"And a man was killed horrifically," Martin's tone shortened as he responded to what he considered Freeborn's selfish remark. "We need to know the exact sequence of events."

"All I know is that the paper got a call from a man about a half past four in the afternoon on Saturday and that the man claimed to have found a mutilated man's body at Dukes Mound hidden in some bushes. He said that he had informed the police, but that for a fee he would give the paper all the details of where the body was and that it was badly cut up; he even claimed to have pictures of the corpse."

"Go on," Martin said.

"Well," said Freeborn. "As I have already said, this man wanted money for the information, and he also wanted to retain his anonymity."

"So did he give anyone who works for the newspaper his name?" Martin interrupted.

"No, no," Freeborn went on. "I never actually met or saw him. I was told on the phone he had spoken to one of the senior reporters at the paper and had struck a deal with him."

At this point, the young female detective addressed her boss. "I have already arranged for a Metropolitan officer to go and get a statement from the senior reporter Mr. Freeborn just mentioned sir," she said. "It was him I spoke to at the paper who finally gave me Mr. Freeborn's contact details."

"Go on, Mr. Freeborn," Martin said.

"Well," Freeborn added. "The deal he did with the paper just meant my going to a phone box by the Palace Pier. I was told I must get there at about five p.m. and there would be a carrier bag in the phone box with a camera in it. I was to take the camera and leave an envelope containing five hundred pounds under the shelf in the phone box."

"Go on," Martin said.

"Well, when I got to the phone box the bag and camera were there, so I put the envelope with the money as requested and then came straight home."

"So you didn't wait to see if anyone came to collect the money?" Martin asked in a desperate tone. "That could have been our killer."

"No, no. I was so excited to have got the camera and knew this was going to be a big story." Freeborn's face dropped in a sudden realisation of the facts. "It never occurred to me that it could have been the killer that was leaving the camera for me," Freeborn added. "I just got carried away by the story. Oh God!"

"So, nobody got the name of the informant at all," Martin said exasperated.

"No," Freeborn said. "It does not work like that in this business. Nobody wants to give names; it's all about the money."

"Your paper was taking a chance, that's a lot of money to hand over with a risk of getting no story or anything in return," Martin retorted.

"Yes I know," Freeborn replied. "But the informant gave quite a detailed account of the injuries on the body and we covered the murder at the Queens Road railway station and heard rumours that the body there was mutilated, so they took a chance."

"You should have informed us about the drop off as we are desperate to talk to this man," Martin said. "I cannot rule out us taking action against you and your newspaper for obstructing police in their enquiries," his voice was raised in frustration.

"You know it doesn't work like that, chief inspector," Freeborn responded. "It would have cost me my job, but in truth, I was so keen to get the story, that I did not even think about it or the consequences." Freeborn's expression changed and with a rush of enthusiasm, he said, "I still have the camera, would that help?" his voice was now racing.

"What here?" Martin said.

"Yes," the journalist replied. "I came home with it and downloaded the pictures. They were sent to head office by email, along with the article I wrote."

"Well, finally some good news." This was just the bit of fortune the detective chief inspector needed. "What about the carrier bag the camera was in?" Martin said.

"No, I threw that, but I'll get the camera now; it's in my study."

Martin almost shouted his response. "No leave it, don't touch it anymore, we will get a scene of crime officer to come here now and see if we can get any prints from it. They will need to take your prints as well, Mr. Freeborn, to eliminate them; let's just hope the informant's prints are still on the camera somewhere."

Freeborn was still trembling but felt he had in some small way redeemed himself. "I just didn't think," he said. "I just wanted the story so badly."

"Right, Mr. Freeborn, at least we now have the camera. I will leave Detective Constable Thomas here. She will take a full statement from you. She will also wait here to see the scenes of crime officers when they arrive." Martin turned to his detective constable. "Are you alright here, Becky? I need to get that camera looked at as soon as possible. When the S.O.C.O. officers come, get them to give you the make, model and serial numbers from the camera. As soon as you have them, ring them through to Dave Smith and tell him to see if he can trace where the camera was sold, and more importantly, who bought it. The time is getting on and I need to get back to 'the nick' and see if Sergeant Carter has any information on our other lead. I had hoped he would have rung me by now, we still have so much to do." Just as Martin finished the sentence the phone in his pocket rang. "I have got to take this," he said getting up. "Excuse me." He picked the car keys up from the table, put his hand over the speaker part of his phone and said, "Get the S.O.C.O. officer to drop you back at 'the nick', Becky. See you later."

"Okay, sir."

The chief inspector moved his hand from the speaker of his phone. "Martin," he said as he shut the front door. He could see from the number calling that it was not his sergeant but D.C. Hopkins. "Yes, Tony," he said.

"I have some good news," Hopkins told his boss. "The Royal Sussex County Hospital, having checked their records has confirmed they have some Dizampathene missing. It seems, also, that it is not just this drug that is missing either. I have a small list. There is more information on these missing drugs, sir, but I need to talk with you face to face," the detective constable said.

"Right," Martin said. "I'm on my way back to 'the factory'; let's meet up there. I'll ring Sergeant Carter and see how he is getting on; hopefully, we are getting somewhere at last!"

It was late that afternoon when Martin returned to the station. As he walked into the incident room, Martin saw Sergeant Carter writing on one of the large whiteboards. "Hello, sir. How did you get on?"

"Bloody journalists, John," Martin said. "But I want to know what happened with you first."

"Yes sorry, governor," Carter replied. "I have not managed to speak to the young man yet. He is one Andrew Holt, aged twenty-seven; he has no real previous just a conviction for actual bodily harm when he was twenty-three – a pub brawl, hence us having his D.N.A. on our database. He now works as a fisherman and is out on a trawler; according to his girlfriend, he will be back first thing tomorrow morning."

"Okay, John, let's keep an open mind on him; he is not going to be killing anyone if he is at sea."

"The girlfriend said he won't be home until at least eight o'clock tomorrow morning. She said she would be at work by then. She can't get a message to him because he doesn't take his mobile phone on the fishing boat, so if we are waiting for him at his home address before eight in the morning, we should be able to pick him up without spooking him, if he indeed has anything to hide."

"Well, I'm not taking his lack of guilt for certain until I have spoken to him; after all, his blood was still found at the crime scene," Martin added. "But I just don't have that 'itch' that he is our man."

"What's your news, sir?" Carter enquired.

"Well, John, it appears our friends in the media may have obstructed our enquiry in the search for a sensational story. But although they do not have a name for their informant as they implied our local friendly nervous journalist does have the informant's camera. S.O.C.O. are on their way to the reporter's home now, and Becky is there getting a statement from him and all the details of the camera. She is going to pass them on to Dave Smith. Where is he by the way?"

"Oh, having a leak, sir."

"Oh, okay. I'll have a chat with him when he gets back. Tracing that camera is very important. I want him working on that as a priority."

"Okay, sir. Well if I see him first, I'll tell him."
"Thanks, John."

The sergeant raised his eyebrows, "Let's hope for our sake our informant was stupid enough to leave his prints on the camera," he replied.

"If he's our killer, I think he would have worn gloves or wiped it down. This one is not just a bastard, he's a clever bastard," Martin said.

As their conversation came to an end, D.C. Hopkins came back into the room. "Right, we need to talk Tony. I want you to hear this as well, John, so go and find Dave Smith, get him working on the camera and then come to my office. While we are waiting get three coffees, Tony, will you, and meet us in there."

"Yes, of course, sir."

D.C. Hopkins came back into the office with three coffees from the machine in the corridor. Carter and Martin were chatting intently about the day's events. "Grab a chair, Tony," Martin said. "And let's have a drink, I'm parched."

With all three men sat around the chief inspector's desk, Martin said. "Right, Tony, so drugs are missing at the hospital?"

"Yes, sir," Hopkins replied. "I have the report from the hospital infirmary; they have a number of different drugs that seem to have gone missing."

"Don't they have a controlled drug register?" Martin said.

"Yes, sir," the detective replied. "There is a controlled drug register. All drugs have to be signed in and out from two large locked controlled drug cabinets. Following our request one of the pharmacists undertook a controlled drug balance, which they do fairly regularly once a month anyway, and on the check, the missing Dizampathene was flagged up. Whoever has taken it knows how to beat the system; it all looked in order to the pharmacist at first," he said.

"How much was missing?" Carter enquired.

"According to the pharmacist, there were five ten ml phials of thirty mg Dizampathene missing. There is a senior pharmacist dedicated only to running the controlled drug cabinets and allocations for the same, but he is on holiday this week. The lady I saw is Miss Cathy Purnell and she only covers for him when he is on days off or holidays. When she double-checked the records against actual stock she was shocked to find the drug missing. And it was not just that drug, others were missing in various quantities; the names are in the report she gave me but I cannot pronounce them," Hopkins said and laughed. "The hospital is now taking this theft seriously enough to launch an enquiry."

"I should bloody think so," Martin said.

"It seems the only way to get access to the controlled drug cabinets is to use a key which the senior dedicated pharmacist has on his or her person all the time; it is not an easy thing at all to get to these drugs," Hopkins added.

"Right, we need to talk to the regular dedicated senior pharmacist, Tony. Perhaps he can shed some light on the missing drugs. Find out where he is. If he is only on holiday locally get hold of him and get a statement from him. The missing drugs must have been taken by someone at the hospital and we need to find out who it is!"

"I'm on that, sir. I have already informed the hospital that I will need to speak to him. He is only on holiday at home I have ascertained. I have tried to ring him there but he was out. But I will get hold of him."

"Yes, right," Martin said. "Get him to meet you at the hospital tomorrow morning. I don't care if he's on holiday. Have you anything to add, John?" Martin said involving his sergeant in the conversation.

"No, governor, but that pharmacist needs seeing as soon as possible."

"Okay," Martin said. "This case feels like two steps forward and three steps back, but we are slowly making headway. Make sure we all put our intelligence on the boards in the incident room and I want a full written report by you passed to D.C. Smith, Tony. I am just going to write my notes up. Okay, let's get back to it."

After finishing writing his reports up and juggling some other more mundane paperwork, Martin returned to the briefing room. He had a tray of sandwiches; it was now eighteen-hundred hours. "Comforts for the troops," he said. "How are you two getting on with your reports?"

"Nearly done, sir," both his sergeant and D.C. Hopkins replied.

"The others will all be back here shortly," Martin said. "It's only an hour until we go off duty. Let's see what S.O.C.O. said to Becky when she gets back." It was only ten minutes later that D.C. Thomas got back to the briefing room followed shortly by D.C.s Andrews, Fuller and Lewis. Slowly the whole room was filled with the complete team of detectives. "Help yourselves to sandwiches and then settle down for the day de-brief.

"Okay, so what did S.O.C.O. say in the end, Becky?" Martin enquired.

"That's why I have been so long," the detective said. "Nothing definite; they have partial prints. But they have taken the camera back to the lab for further analysis and they will have a full report for us tomorrow. I have passed all the camera details to D.C. Smith."

"Yes, I have got them, governor. The serial numbers are being traced, but it's unlikely anyone has a record of sales of that camera; it's a relatively old model," the detective added.

"Okay, anyone anything to add?" The room silenced. "Make sure all your reports are up to date and on the boards, or in Dave Smith's in tray," Sergeant Carter said.

"Okay, people," Martin added. "Let's just have a quick recap and we will call it a day… the public hotline gets opened tomorrow, and all hell is certainly going to break loose."

CHAPTER ELEVEN

Jack sat in the armchair at Compton Street. He was now well aware of the media attention his killings were evoking; he also knew that in every century the press could and did influence the populous. If an atmosphere of terror reigned, Jack's ego was stroked. Jack was astute enough to realise that there were also going to be many pretenders to his crown. And he was right, since announcing and opening a direct call line for information on the murders, the police had been swamped by people claiming to have seen, or even be, the so-called press alter ego 'The Brighton Ripper'. Jack's status as 'The Ripper' was important to him; he wanted to be remembered, feared and revered. He also knew the press involvement and even the possibility of vigilantes on the streets, inhibited and stifled the police in their collation of intelligence. Such mass hysteria diluted their already overstretched manpower and resources and Jack enjoyed watching the internal wrangling and ensuing power struggle, as he sought to bring chaos to their order. This confusion and lack of cohesion aided Jack in the one thing he based his whole reputation on, the ability to never be apprehended. Jack was very clever, he had seen the leading member of the local community Councillor Morgan's press releases, and he knew reading between the lines, that this police adversary could be used in his campaign of terror. Jack sat in Compton Street, the time he thought to exacerbate the situation had arrived and he had a cunning devious plan of inexplicable evil intent, to do just that.

Jack had been in almost a stupor for two days since his last killing but he had gotten over that drained tiredness and seemed revived. He had a renewed sense of purpose once again and had changed his clothes. Having redressed himself, Jack placed the blood-spattered clothing he had just taken off into the grate in the front room of the house at Compton Street adding it to some of his stained clothing already there. After dousing all the items on the fire heavily with paraffin he had found in an old can, he struck a match and set them all alight. He stood and stared into the flickering flames and then shuddered again violently. He turned around and walked out of the door of Compton Street heading purposefully down the road and clutching a small shiny laminated card in his right hand. He stopped at the corner of the road and went into a public phone box situated there. He raised the card that he had in his right hand whilst he punched some numbers into the dial on the phone with his other hand. The card was one Jack had acquired during his early days of exploration in the town, which was advertising the services of a local male prostitute. Jack had discovered some of the city's prostitutes left a few of their so-called 'business cards' in the numerous public phone boxes scattered in the city centre and beyond, and he had over a short time collected many such cards.

"Okay, so you will meet me at the old disused gent's toilet in Kemp Town. Yes, I know the ones," Jack said as he finalised the meeting and venue with the unsuspecting young man chatting to him. "Yes, yes I'll have the money," he added. "See you there tomorrow afternoon at four o'clock sharp, my name?" This threw

Jack for just a moment. He had not expected to be asked his name and it had caught him a little unawares, but he was very sharp of wit. "Yes Jacob," he said. "Jacob is my name."

Jack smiled to himself as he left the phone box and headed back to Compton Street. Once there he went straight for his Gladstone bag. As he lifted it from the table he shook violently again, as if with lustful excitement. He drew a deep breath and gathered himself before opening the bag. Carefully, he took out the precious leather-wrapped surgical tools he cherished with such care and opened and inspected them. Delicately, and with much precision, he cleaned the now coagulated dried blood from each of the many instruments before placing them back neatly into each pouch. Then he went over to the table on which the Gladstone bag had previously been placed. He opened one of the small drawers housed in the front of the table and took out a phial of human blood, a crisp white newly laundered square cloth, one handkerchief, a pair of long surgical-style gloves, a folded up piece of paper and two long lengths of the previously cut rough coarse heavy duty string. He reached underneath the table and took the man-bag he had used in both previous killings and placed all these items into it, as well as the now re-rolled leather holder which contained the pristine and newly cleaned surgical tools.

This action complete, he returned to the drawer again and unpacked a new syringe from its packet and took out a ten ml phial of the Dizampathene. Carefully, he filled the syringe and then placed it gently into his coat pocket. He shut the drawer on the small table and went back over to the Gladstone bag which he closed and placed back up on the table. These actions were all now a well-rehearsed ritual for Jack and, as such, quite deliberately and methodically undertaken. He was ready to kill again, but before that, he needed another good night's rest so he settled back into the tatty armchair and closed his eyes.

The next day Jack left Compton Street at just after three in the afternoon. He closed the door and set off walking quickly. Jack seemed to know his route without hesitation and it took him very little time to reach his destination despite it being quite a walk from Compton Street to Kemp Town. A murky, steadily thickening fog had started to descend inexplicably during Jack's journey, and it now hung in the air. As he drew nearer the disused toilets, Jack could see a young man loitering there. The smartly presented lad had a pink handkerchief hanging loosely from his right-side trouser pocket, the indication that he was working. Jack walked directly up to him. "I rang you," he said.

"Yes, Jacob isn't it? Okay, you got the money?" the young man said.

"Jacob?" Jack repeated quietly, paused for a moment, and without giving himself away said. "Oh, Jacob yes, and of course I have the money." He recalled that Jacob was the name he had given as his own on the phone when he had spoken to the young prostitute earlier and he pulled a small roll of twenty-pound notes which were inside his trousers just into view of the young man.

"It's in here then," the young prostitute said. "Follow me."

The pair disappeared into a small dirty, litter-ridden alley, which led to what once was the opening into the now-disused public toilet. There was a rusty heavy metal barred gate with a large brass padlock on it which the young man opened with a long gold key he pulled from his pocket. "My own private office in here," he said as he pulled the gate open. "My uncle you see, he's the caretaker, so I get the key. It's private," he said. "We will be locked in here so no fear of getting caught in the act!" The young man's blue eyes twinkled as he looked at Jack. He had no idea of the grave nature of what he had just said. "You don't smile a lot do you?" the young man added, as he locked the gate shut again with the pair now both securely inside. "But you're handsome, yes, very handsome," he said as he smiled at Jack again.

Inside the old toilet building, there was a lot of graffiti and tags and these were spray painted in a rainbow of colours on the crumbling and tatty internal walls. A few used condoms littered the grey cold concrete floor, but overall the room was clean considering it had once been a well-used public toilet. There was a row of five heavily pitted mirrors against the far wall under which was a row of chipped and heavily stained hand basins. The young man pointed the long row of old mirrors out to Jack who stood motionless. "The men like the mirrors," he said. "They like to watch exactly what I'm doing with them in the reflection." He laughed and added, "You got the money then?"

"Yes here," said Jack. "Come and get it." He pulled the roll of the twenty- pound notes from his trouser pocket and handed them to his unsuspecting victim.

"Right, sir," the lad said almost in jest. "Shall I take your coat then?"

Jack removed his coat and handed it to the lad, and as he did so, he slipped the small syringe from his coat pocket and expertly concealed it in his right hand. His eyes blackened, the pupils an indication of his now internal raging desire to kill. The young man took the coat, folded it and still with no idea of the gravity of the situation he was in, turned his back on Jack to put the coat down. Suddenly, and without any warning for his victim, Jack who had been almost statuesque up until this moment violently grabbed the young man from behind. He covered his victim's mouth completely with his large left hand and drove the syringe that he had so skilfully hidden in his right hand into the young man's neck. He easily overpowered his much slimmer and smaller victim who was already starting to be paralysed by the fast-acting Dizampathene. The flailing young man's muffled voice could barely be heard through Jack's sizeable left hand. Jack soon felt the lad's panicked resistance against him reducing and finally, the struggling ceased as the Dizampathene took full effect. This frenetic initial activity over, Jack let go of his victim and as he did so, his body fell hard to the cold concrete floor. The young man was paralysed, fully conscious and aware of his surroundings, he was just unable to move or speak. Jack seemed to return to a calm almost hypnotic state. He knew he was relatively safe in this secured and self-contained environment and was unlikely to be disturbed. His methodical murderous appalling act could begin.

Jack knelt beside the prostrated lad and opened the man bag with no great sense of urgency. He removed the long pair of latex surgeon's gloves and pulled them one at a time onto his hands and up his hairy forearms. The hairs on his arms were noticeably erect and stood on end with his body once again being stimulated by the excitement of this whole murderous experience. This act completed, he took the pristine white square of cloth from the man-bag and unfolded it neatly on the ground a little way away from the helpless body of his victim. Having taken the time to gently flatten the cloth exactingly to the floor, Jack took a deep breath and as he did so he shuddered violently with blood lust. "Do call out for help if you can, although nothing can save you," he said through a small wicked smile and in a dark demonic tone, the whispered phrase only muttered to add to the terror of his helpless captive.

Jack turned to the man-bag again, he took out the two long pieces of coarse string and the leather cylinder which contained the surgical instruments that were so very precious to him. He untied and unrolled the pouch and then, with his eyes blackening further, he took the largest scalpel from its pocket. With precision, but in a violent manner, he cut the young man's clothes from him, only putting down the sharp glistening scalpel to turn his victim's recumbent body over and to remove the final items of clothing and footwear which had not been released by the frenetic cutting. Jack paused for a moment. He carefully picked up the young man's shoes and placed them in an exacting fashion neatly beside the motionless body of his victim. He grabbed forcefully at the man's legs, pulled them back in a brutal fashion, and tied them tightly. Immediately after his victim's limbs were tied the skin blackened on them; the coarse string constricting and cutting into his soft flesh.

Jack turned his attention to the young man's paralysed hands and arms. He wrenched them awkwardly behind his captive's back before also binding them brutally in a similar fashion to the way he had the lad's ankles. "Must get these things right," he muttered, his madness was almost tangible.

Jack moved the terrified and fully conscious young man's body again and laid it almost in his lap. "It's just me and you now," he said demonically for his victim's benefit, as he picked up the large razor-sharp scalpel from the floor and replaced it neatly into the pocket of the leather pouch. Jack removed the smallest scalpel in his roll of death and concentrated intently once again; he gently brushed each of the young man's nipples to make them pert and then with the skill of a surgeon he expertly removed them, one at a time. Jack carefully placed the nipples onto the white cloth, tilting his head staring and examining them as they stained the crisp white cloth and tainted it with fresh deep red blood. He replaced the small scalpel in the pouch and proceeded to pull the victim away from his lap. The immobile young man was now lying on the floor on his back and his eyes were looking upward fixated with terror.

Having moved his victim to the position he wanted him Jack pulled violently at the front of his victim's hair, tugging it forward until his paralysed captive could see his own naked and exposed midriff. Jack now used his free hand to pick out one of the largest scalpels from the leather pouch and with his eyes blackening further he held it up for his victim to see. He whispered in a quiet but very disturbing voice, "I want you to watch this!" Before he carefully and exactingly pressed the large scalpel deeply into and under the skin, just above his captive's pelvis, and started to slice open the flesh of the motionless young man. He was cutting deliberately, expertly but with more fervour now, forcing the instrument up the whole length of the body of his victim and right up to the start of his sternum. The incision seemed to have no effect at first because of the sharpness of the blade, but when the wound sprang open it transfixed Jack and he became more excited. Jack was frenzied. He viciously forced his hands inside the opened torso and pulled brutally at the exposed internal organs. As he did so the young man's body contorted violently, registering the immense pain of such a violent intrusion. Jack laid the organs now bloodied, grey, and ruptured onto the chest of his victim and squeezed them sharply.

His conquest quivered uncontrollably again with more agonising pain, still fully conscious and trembling with the shock of the terrible wounds. Jack now raised the large blade up, just high enough for his victim to see, and then thrust it forcefully downwards and into the side of his victim's throat just below his ear. He drove it jaggedly across the length of the young man's windpipe, ripping through skin, arteries, sinew and the cartilage of the neck itself, which cracked pitifully as it ruptured. The action of the Dizamapethene stopped the blood pumping from this newly inflicted wound and it just leeched a trickle of constant, black dark blood. Finally, the victim contorted one last time, and he was dead.

Jack by now was devoid of any control of his madness and absorbed totally in his usual merciless full flight of insanity. He moved the sharp blade down and into his victim's groin where he hacked at and removed the genitals. Then in almost a ritual fashion, he held them aloft for a few seconds like a trophy, before ramming them with a huge amount of force into the mouth of the corpse. Jack knew he had the unprecedented luxury at this murder scene of total seclusion and his actions did not have to be as hurried as when he killed in places where he was more likely to be discovered. He took full advantage of this and knew savaging the victim was not a concern here. He was isolated and locked away from the outside world and his psychopathic madness was growing by the minute. His fervour and his uncontrollable shaking also increased alarmingly, as the total depravity running through him drove him on in the manner of the madman he became when he was overtaken by this blood lust.

Jack ripped away parts of the small and large intestines and then took his scalpel again and despite his increasing frenzy cut expertly, but also frantically, at the now completely exposed internal organs. He skilfully removed both of the victim's kidneys and cut out nearly the entirety of his liver as well as extracting part of the pancreas. His whole body and frame by this point were almost fitting with lustful exuberance and his cutting was become more ragged. He was decimating the entirety of the body lying before him.

Jack slashed at the victim making several further incisions in the face and chest, before he shook again, this time with unprecedented violence. Exhausted, Jack slumped suddenly forward, the madness driving him almost visibly leaving his being as if it were exorcised by these last cuts to the now dismembered and destroyed torso. He trembled violently one last time and then, having seemingly gathered himself a little, he took a huge gasp of air and, now calming, replaced the large scalpel into its precise pocket of the pouch and for a moment stared intently at his still trembling hands.

A hypnotic tranquillity started to come over Jack, it could almost be visibly seen to sweep over him. He was losing the blackness in his eyes and they were reverting to a softer dark colour. This said he was still impervious and unmoved by the scene of absolute and total carnage which lay before him. Jack gently took the smallest scalpel and with expert precision, deliberately carved three short vertical straight lines deeply into the victim's left cheek. His shaking and the violence of his madness, by this point, had ended.

Jack focused again, coldly reached for the man-bag and took out the phial inside it containing the purchased blood. He placed it onto the rippled concrete floor which was already heavily stained and soiled with an ever-increasing amount of dark black, sanguine fluid seeping from his victim's wounds. He pulled off one of his gloves and put that on the floor. Jack then poured some of the blood from the newly opened phial onto the glove and dragged the lifeless fingers of his victim's right hand through it, ensuring some blood went up and under the actual fingernails. This completed Jack suddenly, and without any other previous expression of real emotion, gave a dark demonic smile, this smile lasted just seconds and he then stared dispassionately once more at the wreckage of human form lying before him.

Jack still knew he would not be disturbed. His well-rehearsed death ritual had changed and would again as he removed the victim's genitals, from the mouth of the corpse. This act of further depravity was difficult because, in his frenetic madness, he had initially forced the genitals into the oral cavity with such venom. Indeed, as he removed them the skin and the flesh on them tore as they were cut and ripped apart further by the mangled victim's teeth. Finally removed, Jack inspected them almost clinically. He smiled wickedly to himself again and put them carefully onto the cold concrete floor. Jack took a clean white handkerchief from the man-bag and wrapped the ripped and bloodied genitals carefully in it. The black blood immediately leeched into the white crisp newly laundered cloth. He now placed the filled handkerchief gently back into the man-bag, before packing away his instruments of death. Next Jack removed a folded-up piece of white paper from his bag. He placed the still folded paper onto the ground exactly beside the mutilated torso, this time using one of the kidneys he had cut away so expertly from the victim to hold it in place.

Jack now turned his attention to his victim's clothing. He picked up his ravaged conquest's trousers and with the hand that was still gloved casually looked through the young man's pockets for the key to allow his escape. By chance Jack came across the money he had given the young prostitute earlier and with another black smile he put it back into his own trouser pocket. "You will not be needing that," he muttered insanely to himself. Then he carried on going through the young man's pockets until he found the precious gold-coloured padlock key.

The key recovered, Jack stood up and in doing so he caught sight of himself in one of the five pitted mirrors. He walked over to it and stared fixedly into his dark eyes that were reflected back at him. Jack was standing gazing at his reflection for some time, suddenly this derealisation was gone and he was back in the room. He turned away from the mirrors and moved back towards his victim. With his gloved hand still holding the key Jack reached into the thick, black blood now pooling from the destroyed body. This sea of black, bloody tar was slowly covering the entirety of the concrete floor surrounding the dehumanised torso.

Jack stood back up and moved over to the mirrors and with his hand trembling again wrote across the glass in blood and with quite deliberate large letters:

JACK IS BACK

Jack shuddered violently again. "Time to go," he said. "Time to go," he repeated madly to himself.

Jack left the scene precisely as he wanted it to look, with the victim's shoes neatly presented beside the mangled body and his surgically removed nipples symmetrically placed on the blood-stained white square cloth positioned a little way from the corpse, exactly as he had, in fact, at the other two previous awful murders. His glove now removed and with everything required packed away, Jack reached for his coat from the floor. He unfolded the coat with a gentle precision and put it on. He picked up his man bag and hung it loosely on his left shoulder. One last double-check, just to be sure nothing had been forgotten, and Jack walked out of the toilets, carefully ensuring no one was nearby to see him leave.

The roads were quiet as Jack made his way back to the security of Compton Street and he stopped only once on his journey, to drop the gold padlock key to the gent's toilet gate down a roadside drain. He was totally exhausted from the killing, but his being tingled with the thrill of his murderous actions. "I must get home," he whispered madly to himself. "I must get home."

CHAPTER TWELVE

The officers were assembled in the all too familiar major incident room as Martin and Carter came in first thing for the early morning briefing. There was the usual ripple of low mumbling voices mentioning everything from the case, to who was the local source of gossip in 'the nick' at that time. "Right, everyone, come on, listen up," Martin said. "I know this is a tiring case," he added. "Any quality telephone leads have been few and far between but it's all about processes of elimination at the moment. Our killer is still out there and it's very much cat and mouse at this present time."

The chief inspector paused for a moment and continued: "So, the 'S.O.C.O.' report has come back in on the camera our reporter Mr. Freeborn had tucked away. No full prints and a complete dead end on that so far, but we are still trying serial numbers and tracing the long shot of when it was bought and where. We have been liaising closely with the Royal Sussex County Hospital and they are conducting their own enquiry into the missing drugs, so I am hopeful for some sort of a lead there. Apart from that it's all back to where we were with usual enquiries etc, etc. Does anyone have any questions?" Martin asked as a young constable came rushing into the room.

"Another one, sir; there has been another killing sir," the young police constable said, breathing heavily after his exertion of getting to the incident room in such a hurried fashion. "I was told to come and tell you," he gasped. "A caretaker found what was left of the body of his nephew just now, in an old disused public toilet in Kemp Town."

"Oh for fuck's sake," Martin sighed. "Right, people, you know what you are on, let's get to it. John, you are with me."

By the time Martin and Carter arrived at the disused toilets, the area was already alive with police. Cordons were being put up and several forensic incident tents had already been erected. As Martin and Carter walked into the ensuing chaos, they saw an ambulance crew attending to an elderly man who was sitting on a small wall nearby.

"Hello, governor," the uniformed sergeant in charge of the scene said. He gestured towards the old man sitting with the ambulance crew. "That's the informant; it was his nephew he found inside, or what's left of him," he added. "The lad was a young male prostitute, Marcus Robertson. Believe it or not, his uncle is the caretaker for the public toilets and he used to let Marcus have a key to bring clients here."

"Bloody hell," Martin said. "For money I suppose."

"Yes, governor I guess so. The old guy was haemorrhaging information and he was in such a state of shock I thought we'd better get him stable before asking him anything else. To be honest, sir, I've been inside, and I've never seen anything like this; it's terrible, terrible, in there."

"Thanks, sergeant. Okay, we'll take it from here."

"Oh, and there is something else, sir. Something I think only you and Sergeant Carter should see. I'm the only person other than the old man who could have seen it. I kept everyone else out of the room. You will see why when I show you."

"Well, what is it?" Martin snapped.

"Come with me, sir, I'll show you," the uniformed sergeant said. Martin, Carter and the uniformed skipper went in through the half-opened door.

"Dear God," Martin said. Both he and Carter were openly, visibly shocked at the carnage that greeted them.

"Over there, sir, on the glass," the sergeant said. The three men looked over to the mirrors. Clearly written in blood were the words:

JACK IS BACK

"Oh, fucking hell," Martin said. "Right, let's get out of here and get Marshall and the forensic boys in," he added. "I don't need to tell you, sergeant, but not a word of this to anyone. Oh, and well done for using your initiative. Okay, John," Martin spoke quietly to his sergeant who was still obviously disturbed by what he had just witnessed. "Now this madman thinks it is a game. Paper poems are bad enough but he's taunting us. This bloody 'Jack the Ripper' thing could get out of hand. We need a lid on this as soon as possible. Let's see if the uncle is fit to be interviewed quickly. What is his name, sergeant?"

"Oh, his name's Michael. Michael Simpson, sir."

"Hi, Marshall," Carter said.

"I've just got here," she said. "Is it our friend again?"

"Yes, I'm afraid so and just a heads-up, Mary. This one is terrible and he's writing his messages in blood now as well," Martin said. Even he was still shaken by what he had just witnessed.

"Oh, okay, goodness," Marshall replied. "And the

writing in the blood. What as well as or instead of poems?" The poems intrigued her as they were such an unusual twist and she had never discovered anything like them before at any of the many murder scenes she had witnessed.

"I don't know, Mary," the detective chief inspector said. "We didn't notice one, but that is unsurprising, it is carnage in there. The victim has been destroyed this time."

"Okay," Marshall said now putting on her forensic clothing. "Well, my team will go in do our usual and lock the scene down. As soon as I have completed my initial inspection and I'm happy the 'S.O.C.O.' lads are finished with the body, I'll get him to the morgue. Should have an initial autopsy report for you late afternoon," she added.

"Let's get suited and booted, John. We had better have a proper look at the scene. We must be due a lucky break in this case," Martin said. His voice was drained of enthusiasm.

The two detectives now dressed in forensic suits went into the disused toilets with Marshall, who followed them in. The scene that met the three of them was horrific; the grey rippled concrete was saturated in the blackest coagulated blood and thick clots had formed around and on the victim's torso itself. The intestines, as with the other murders, had been laid onto the chest and stomach of the corpse and their tube-like form was going from a greying to a dark, charcoal colour. These intestines also had been ruptured by their man- handling during the violent assault and their content had escaped and was seeping and mixing with the thick, black blood. The room had a heady pungent stench of odious bodily gases mixed with the aroma of death.

"Never pretty these, are they?" Marshall said.

"Sickening," Martin replied.

"Something different about this one from just the devastated torso, though," Sergeant Carter interjected. "Look at the victim's mouth, governor." Martin and to a lesser extent Marshall had been focusing on the ghoulish writing that decorated the pitted, rusty mirrors on the far wall. Indeed, the torso was such a mangled wreck the diligent sergeant had done well to notice the mouth was torn and open but that no genitals were present in either it or the throat.

Marshall took a closer look, her expert eye engaged enquiringly in the oral cavity of the corpse. "Something has been forced into the mouth and removed," Marshall said. "There is still an amount of torn flesh on the victim's teeth. I will need to examine the torso in more detail at the morgue, but for now, if the genitals have been removed, they quite possibly are no longer with the corpse."

"My God," Martin said. "Come on, John. I've seen enough I need some clean air," he said to Carter.

"What about the note? There is one under the corpse I can see it," Marshall added. "Oh God," she said. "There is a kidney on it I think."

"I'm not in the mood for more bloody poetry," Martin said. "I need some thinking time." He knew by now the note was not going to reveal any major new inspiring item of evidential value and the shock of the loss of another young life in such an act of absolute barbarism, he had found hard to take. He almost felt responsible. "I'm going to catch this fucking bastard, John," he said. "Mark my fucking words!"

The two detectives went out of the squalid toilet. "Bugger, there is my phone," Martin said. "John, you go and chat with the uncle and see if he has any more information. I need to take this call, it could be important."

"Okay, sir."

"Yes, Martin," the detective chief inspector sighed. "What, hang on a minute, I can't hear you properly." The whole area by this time was swarming with uniformed police. Some of the officers at the front of the cordon were being harassed and jostled by members of the public and several interested news reporters who had gotten wind of the potential of another murder.

"That's better," Martin said now having moved to where he could hear more clearly. "What, you are at the hospital now?"

"Yes, sir, and they have come up with a name; a student doctor who had access to both the blood phials and the controlled drug cabinets."

"Yes, yes, of course, I want to know who he is. I don't care if they are not certain we have nothing else to go on. Find him and bring him into 'the nick' now. Yes, arrest him if he won't come off his own back. I'll take the responsibility. See you back at 'the factory'. Oh and, Tony, once you have nicked him call the communications room. Get them to send a uniformed officer down to the backyard to make sure no reporters are down there. Press reports and pictures of suspects are two things we don't fucking need."

"Finished, governor," Carter said as he walked back up to his chief inspector. "The uncle has nothing new for us. Nothing at all and he's devastated, totally devastated."

"Forget the uncle, John. D.C. Hopkins has got a new lead at the hospital, a student doctor no less. The only person who according to the hospital records has had access to the blood of all patients whose bloods we have found at each crime scene and who has authorised access to the controlled drug cabinets; he is being brought in now, at last something." Martin's voice was raised in the desperate hope of some small breakthrough. "We can't do any more here, John. Let's get back to 'the nick' and have a chat with our student doctor friend. Marshall has got this covered, she knows this case inside and out," he added.

When Martin and Carter got back to the John Street police station, D.C. Hopkins had already got the young student Doctor Kowalski locked up in a cell in the custody suite and Hopkins was in a C.I.D. office busily writing his basic arrest statement.

"How did our young doctor react to being brought in?" Martin asked. He was hoping the shock of him having been arrested might have drawn a confession from the young man of some sort.

"Scared, a little indignant, but tight-lipped, he didn't say much and I thought it better you questioned him. I didn't want to miss anything important, so I didn't quiz him, sir," Hopkins replied.

"What did you 'nick' him for?" Martin asked. "We don't want to give too much away at this time," he added.

"No, sir, I guessed that. I arrested him on suspicion of theft of controlled drugs," Hopkins said.

"Oh well done Tony. Sergeant Carter and I are going to chat to Kowalski in a minute, so bring us up to speed with what the hospital said." Before D.C. Hopkins could say anything further D.C. Thomas put her head around the door of the small C.I.D. office.

"Our fisherman," she said. "He has a watertight alibi," her words were deliberate and very typical of sarcastic police humour, a coping mechanism for most. "Yes, a watertight alibi for all the killings. He has either been at sea at the specific times of the murders. Or not at home and in the Royal Sussex County Hospital having an operation on his mouth. Coincidently, sir, they did take some blood from him, I asked him. It's all in a statement in your office."

"Oh, great work, Becky," Martin replied.

"Right, what did the hospital say about Doctor Kowalski, Tony?" Martin focussed his attention again on D.C. Hopkins.

"Well, I gave them a couple of names we had from the blood Marshall found at the scenes and they both had samples of blood taken at the hospital by, guess who?"

"I haven't got time for bloody guessing games, detective, just tell me!" Martin replied, frustrated.

"Kowalski," the detective constable said, "our student Doctor Kowalski."

"And the controlled drug cabinet?" Martin asked.

"Yes, he has had access to it, albeit limited, but has signed to say he has withdrawn certain drugs from the cabinet on at least three occasions and, though not the drugs we are interested in, he could have got access to Dizampathene phials, the hospital pharmacist said. Also, other hospital records show it was only Kowalski who was present at every specific point we were interested in. It may very well be a coincidence, but he is a common denominator. Whether this has any bearing at all, sir, he is openly gay and mixes with lots of persons in the circle of our victims."

"Right," Martin said. "We need to talk to this

Kowalski and we need to talk to him now! John, before we do can you go into my office, have a look at that report on the fisherman from the hospital that Becky put in and see if our student Doctor Kowalski was the doctor who took his blood sample."

Sergeant Carter disappeared, reappearing after just a few minutes with a huge beaming smile on his face. "Good hunch, governor. Yes, it states in the report that Kowalski was indeed the doctor who took the fisherman's blood sample!"

Martin and Carter spent a short time together gathering all the facts they had to date and then went down the stairs that led to the station's custody block. Having seen the custody sergeant, a jailor brought the anxious and nervous Kowalski up to the interview room where the two police detectives sat patiently, but keenly, waiting. After identifying themselves as present and getting the young student Doctor Kowalski to identify himself to the tape machine, they repeated to him that he was still under caution and that the interview would be recorded. "Do you want a solicitor?" Martin asked the visibly scared and agitated young man.

"No, I haven't done anything wrong," Kowalski pleaded. "Why have you brought me here? Why?"

Martin and Carter outlined firstly the theft of the drugs and also the discrepancies in the controlled drug balance and then asked the young man to give an account of where he had been on the times and dates of the murders, none of which had he been at work on and none of which he said could be corroborated. At this point of the interview, they were careful not to reveal that these times or dates were specific to any murders having taken place.

"I spend a lot of time studying," Kowalski pleaded. "Why are you asking me these things?"

Martin changed the questioning slightly. "Are you right-handed or left-handed Mr Kowalski?" the detective asked.

"Why would you ask this?" Kowalski replied.

"Answer the question, Doctor Kowalski," the detective said sternly.

"I'm ambidextrous," Kowalski said.

"Oh," Martin went on. "Well, which hand do you prefer to write with? I'm sure you do a lot of writing." The senior detective's questioning was deliberately loaded.

"Only at work," Kowalski said. "And then I always write with my left hand," he added. The two detectives glanced at each other.

"Write me a short sentence on this piece of paper here about the weather," Martin said to the confused Kowalski.

Kowalski picked up the pen and wrote on the paper. Martin turned it around and both he and Sergeant Carter could see the handwriting was similar, but not identical to, the notes they had found at the murders. Undeterred by this small setback, Martin decided it was time to put some pressure on the young doctor. Kowalski could have disguised the writing on the notes they had found Martin thought, but he knew without the writing being identical this line of questioning was at an end for the time being. It was time Martin changed his tactic again.

Martin now gave Kowalski the list of times and dates of the murders again and once again asked Kowalski to give exact details of where he had been and who, if anyone, had been with him to corroborate his account of events.

"I have already told you all this," Kowalski said desperately. "I don't know why you are asking me constantly about these dates and times."

"Well, tell me again," Martin retorted. "Tell me again."

"I don't know. On my own, I think. I'm so confused," Kowalski said as he put his head in his hands. "I was probably studying, I don't know."

The interview which up until now had been fundamentally about the theft of the drugs and some times and places switched, as Martin decided it was time to give the young doctor another harsh jolt and impart some more mental pressure. He said, "Do any of these dates mean anything to you: Wednesday the fifteenth, Saturday the eighteenth, and Wednesday the twenty-second of November? It is important. Three young men were murdered between fourteen-hundred hours and seventeen-hundred hours on these days, Doctor Kowalski."

Kowalski's face drained with a sudden realisation of what the policeman was asking him. "No, no, you cannot think I did that!" he cried. "No, no, not that I didn't, I didn't have anything to do with those killings."

The detective chief inspector went on to outline to the young man the fact that blood had been found at each scene belonging to a patient that Kowalski had taken blood samples from in the hospital and that coupled with the missing drugs put him as their top suspect in the murder case to date.

"I didn't kill anyone, I have not done anything wrong," Kowalski pleaded. "I take blood from people. It is part of my job. Kowalski's pattern of thought changed. "I want a solicitor," he said. "I want a solicitor, you are framing me."

"Yes, we will get you a solicitor, and while we are waiting for one to be appointed for you, we will be searching your student accommodation, Doctor Kowalski," Martin said, deliberately trying to provoke a response from the young man.

"You can't do that," Kowalski replied instinctively.

His reaction excited Martin. The detective was desperate to find some sort of physical evidence to support his instincts that this was his killer and Kowalski seemed extremely nervous at the mere suggestion of his home being searched. "Yes, I can," Martin said. "What am I going to find there, Doctor Kowalski?" Martin stared at the young man, deliberately making eye-to-eye contact with him.

"Nothing, nothing," the young man said quietly. "Nothing at all, I want my solicitor."

With Kowalski now asking for a solicitor Martin knew he had to terminate the interview until one arrived. He also knew the balance of probability of any confession was frustratingly gone. His shock tactic was over and he was still no closer to finding the killer he sought so very desperately. Kowalski by now, though, was both his and Sergeant Carter's first choice of prime suspect, but both knew thinking he was guilty and proving it were two different things. They just hoped searching his home would reveal something of significant evidential value.

With the interview suspended the detective chief inspector and his sergeant headed back upstairs to their own offices. Several hours had passed since they had last been at the awful murder scene in the disused public toilet. "Right, while we are waiting for

Kowalski's brief, let's call all the troops in and have a meeting so we can see where we all are and where we go from here," Martin said.

After several phone calls and radio messages, as well as three or four cups of coffee and a rather uninspiring floppy cheese sandwich from the station bar which Martin and his sergeant had shared, all of the detectives had returned to the station and were buzzing around the incident room.

"We've got a 'body' then," D.C. Smith said to Martin as he walked into the major incident room closely followed by Sergeant Carter.

"Yes we have got a 'body'," Martin said. "But let's start with all your news first." The detective constables relayed their various bits and pieces of information. There were indeed several new suspects and witness sightings to be investigated, but most of them were already known to the detective chief inspector and his sergeant. The only real seemingly concrete lead they still had was Kowalski and the details that the hospital had provided.

"The uncle at the Kemp Town toilets was, as we thought, getting cash for the key that his nephew used," D.C. Thompson reported. "He is in pieces, though, seeing his nephew like that."

"I'm not surprised poor sod," Martin replied. "So, at the moment our best shot at a suspect is our young man in the cell block. Sergeant Carter and I are going to search his property before we continue with the interview. Right, I want D.C.s Thompson, Hopkins and Thomas all on Kowalski. I want to know his background, where he goes, who he has seen, any friends he has, what he has for breakfast, and the works, please. You can decide amongst yourselves who is doing what. He is openly homosexual so check all the bars and clubs and also check for any potential boyfriends or partners. Get the whisper on anything to do with drugs and check once again with the hospital, I want everything they have said checked and cross-referenced. The rest of you keep following up the leads as they arise. Please liaise with Dave Smith if you get anything that is new or even something little that you judge could be important to this case, and let either me or Sergeant Carter know immediately. I trust every one of you, if something doesn't smell right I need to know about it straight away. "

Just as he finished his last sentence the briefing room phone rang. "It's the custody sergeant, sir," John Carter said. "Kowalski is talking to his brief and he has said they will be ready for the interview to resume in about an hour."

"Who is the brief?" Martin asked.

"Oh, it's the duty brief," Carter said "You are not going to like it, it's Sally Jones!"

"Oh, for fucks sake," Martin said. "Yes, just fucking great. Miss bloody dot the, I's and cross the T's herself. Well, let's get this accommodation checked." Martin and Sergeant Carter left the John Street Station with a degree of optimism. Lawfully because Kowalski was under arrest for a serious offence they could search his property. It did involve some extra paperwork, but if they found some crucial evidence the case could be solved. Searching the property would not take long. He had a single room as a student doctor in a small block on the hospital grounds.

It was not long before Martin's frustrations were evident once more. "Nothing, John," Martin said exasperated. "We have been through this place with a fine toothcomb and nothing. Not even a bloody headache tablet, let alone any murder paraphernalia."

"Perhaps he has another address, governor?"

"Well, if he has, I doubt he will tell us. No, John. I think we are screwed, let's get back to 'the factory'."

The two policemen returned to the interview room in the cell block, both with fresh coffee in hand. As they went in the young female solicitor said, "Hello, detective chief inspector; we meet again. No coffee for me, but thank you," she said sarcastically.

Even before the two police officers could go through the formalities of identifying everyone present, Miss Jones spoke: "How did your comprehensive search go?" she gloated. "Did you find your evidence?"

Sally Jones already knew the answer to her rhetorical question from the detective chief inspectors' body language. She had noticed astutely both the officer's quiet demeanour when they had re-entered the room and this coupled with the fact she had chatted extensively to her young client and thought him to be telling the truth, only reinforced this appraisal. "I have chatted to my client, detective chief inspector," she said. "And I feel at this time you have very little to hold him here with, let alone charge him with. I think it would be in everyone's best interests if you released him whilst you, substantiate his lack of any wrongdoing."

"Your client has taken the samples of blood found at the scenes of some particularly gruesome killings," Martin said to the young solicitor.

"Yes, he takes blood samples, chief inspector, he has already told me. He is a doctor. Taking blood is commonly what doctors do. Was my client' blood found at these murder scenes?" Sally Jones said curtly.

"No. But," Martin said.

"No. But, exactly what are you saying, detective chief inspector?" Sally Jones retorted.

The detective chief inspector sighed. He knew she was right at this time, as everything of any evidential value he had was circumstantial and not corroborated. The shocking sight of the awful body the police officer had witnessed at the Kemp Town toilets had, he wondered, made him act in haste in having Kowalski arrested. Martin was just desperate to prevent any further killings. The search of Kowalski's property had revealed nothing apart from what a tidy young man he was and he knew Sally Jones was a worthy adversary and she would have briefed her client well in the short time she had spent with him. Martin had no real hard actual evidence; the little handwriting exercise he had engineered had proven inconclusive and he had relied on Kowalski breaking and confessing, just with the shock of having been arrested. With Miss Jones's attention to detail, one wrong phrase could blow the case against Kowalski altogether, so reluctantly, he agreed to stop the interview from progressing for the time being. "I'd rather Mr Kowalski remained in custody," Martin added with the interview now terminated.

"Oh really detective chief inspector, can I ask you why? Has my law-abiding young student doctor got anything that he needs to hide? I don't think so and I'm sure you wouldn't be foolish enough to suggest he might abscond." The solicitor's words were well-chosen and venomous. "No," she added. "You release him until you have something that you are sure you need to question him about, Detective Chief

Inspector." The solicitor and Kowalski got up to leave the room, "Mr Kowalski is free to go at this time, chief inspector, isn't he?" Miss Jones said. The two policemen remained seated.

"Only two hours until the end of another frustrating shift," Martin said as Kowalski and Miss Jones left the room. "Let's go and see Marshall first thing in the morning, John. And let's hope by then, she's got something more for us to go on," he added.

CHAPTER THIRTEEN

Jack had made it back safely to the security of his Compton Street home. He removed his coat and slumped into the living room armchair. Jack was prostrated by the killings and they dragged every ounce of energy from his body. He still had lots of splatters of blackened blood on his clothing but nothing was more important to him at this time than to sleep. Once he had rested, he knew he would have plenty of time to clean himself up and plan his next instalment of terror for the people of the City of Brighton.

The next morning there was an unusually long briefing at the John Street police station. Martin had to reveal to everyone the details and failure of success in Kowalski's arrest. In addition, the names of suspects appearing on the collator's board were steadily increasing and Martin had to go through all the snippets of information and organise his detectives accordingly. The officers in the case were frantically checking with a growing number of witnesses who thought they may have seen the killer and persons desperate to confess to and win the notoriety of being labelled the so-called 'Brighton Ripper'.

After some time spent catching up on all the reports and with the shift hurrying past, Martin and John Carter took a slow drive to the morgue to see the pathologist Marshall. The pair of detectives, as well as being long-standing work colleagues, had a very close friendship and this slow drive enabled them to share their feelings openly with one another. "I still really think Kowalski is our man," Sergeant Carter said. "It fits, it all fits."

"I know," Martin said. "But we both know in this job nothing is ever as it seems and, with our dear Miss Jones now watching our every move, things just took another frustrating backward turn. There is just something not quite right about this case, John. And that 'Jack Is Back' thing is haunting me. There was something more than sinister in those words."

"They are just the words of a complete nutcase, governor," Carter said.

"Yes, but a nutcase that's running us round in circles at the moment, my old friend," Martin replied.

The pair arrived at the morgue and went straight inside. "Have you got any good news for us?" Carter asked Marshall, practically as soon as they came in through the door.

"Well," Marshall said. "It is the same killer and the same method of operation; he tied the victim up and then surgically removed the nipples and inflicted as much suffering on the helpless and paralysed young man as possible before death," she added. "The same drug Dizampathene in the blood and organs and this time three straight lines were carved deeply into the victim's left cheek. There are though, at this killing, several major differences. The first is the fact that after a full autopsy, I have confirmed the genitals are no longer with the corpse. In addition, all the mutilations have been horrendous at all murders to date by this suspect, but at this killing, as you both bore witness to, the murderer destroyed the corpse.

There was more evidence of savagery in the cutting and opening of the abdomen and the killer treated the body like a cadaver and demonstrated a more in-depth medical knowledge in the precise way the organs were removed. I'm surmising," she added. "And I am hopeful that this extra brutality was only because he was locked in with his victim and thereby had more time and was unlikely to be disturbed. But it could mean our killer is growing in his confidence of not being apprehended, and this new extra viciousness is disturbing me. Then, of course, there's that writing," she said. "'Jack Is Back'. I'm not usually shaken by anything, but I must admit this case has got to me."

"Not you as well, Mary," Sergeant Carter replied. "I have had that from the governor nearly all the way here."

"Well, Mary," Martin went on. "Perhaps our killer is upping the stakes. He is now taking trophies. This does give us some small encouragement. In his taking the genitals, firstly, he is risking carrying and possibly getting caught with them in his possession. He is also spreading our chance of finding some forensic evidence, and only we and the killer know that he has kept the genitals from this corpse. If we have someone confessing who affords us this detail, he must be our man."

"I think he is too clever for that, Tim," Marshall replied.

"Well," John Carter interjected. "Everyone no matter how smart makes a mistake in the end. Murder is never a perfect art," he added.

"Blimey, John," Martin said, the sergeant's remark had lightened the mood slightly. "Profound, but let's hope true. What else have we got, Mary?"

"Well, there was another paper note."

"Okay," Martin replied, puffing out his cheeks in a familiar fashion. "What did this one say?"

"Well, firstly no prints again," she said.

"No surprise there," Carter replied.

"Okay, so here is the verse this time," Marshall said. "It is quite chilling. It reads:

> 'Listen up and pray do tell,
>
> Those who fear, do fear me well,
>
> The doctor operates to save,
>
> For me, the purpose is to fill the grave'."

"So, we know this madman likes to think of himself as 'Jack the Ripper'. He also knows the history of the case. Whoever he is, he is playing games with us. Unlike 'Jack the Ripper' as I said before to John, I intend to catch this bastard," Martin said. "Never doubt that."

"Well," Marshall replied. She could feel the tension grow again in the room and hoped to diffuse it slightly. "Let's look at the facts, the victim, it is confirmed, was Marcus Robertson, twenty-three years of age and a practising homosexual. He was killed approximately between the hours of four and five-thirty p.m. yesterday in the manner of which we now know. His genitals were removed from the torso and have not yet been recovered. Once again he had blood under his fingernails that was not his, and at this time cannot be ruled out as the killer's. More than that and details of just whose blood it is are not yet known to us. It hasn't matched currently on any of the D.N.A. databases."

"Oh well, at least it's not another copper's," Carter interjected.

"Don't even say that," Martin said sharply. "Right the blood; any idea when we will know whose it is?"

"I'll call the hospital in the hope it is another recent patient's, and I should have a result back by nine a.m. tomorrow. I'll call you and I'll send the autopsy report over in the usual manner, okay?"

"Yes, fine thanks," Martin said. "My concern now is the ripper killed five victims as I recall. Our killer started at five cuts into the left cheek of his victims; he is now down to three, which means?"

"Yes," Marshall and Carter said simultaneously. "Two more victims to go," the pair added together. The thought had occurred to them all earlier but none had wanted to be the first to relay it. It only added more stress to an already pressurised case. "We have got to catch this bastard before he kills again," Martin added. "Right back to 'the factory', de-brief the troops and I'm going to the pub. Are you coming, John? I need some thinking time."

"Yes, governor, I'll come," his loyal sergeant replied. He knew his friend needed a bit of extra support during such a stressful time. "I'll ring the wife, it's only shepherd's pie for dinner and it's my dog's favourite," Carter added and laughed. "Funny, you never find a detective with a skinny pet dog," he said still trying to lighten the very strained atmosphere.

"No, you are right there, John," Martin replied. "If this case carries on like this, my friend, yours will have fucking diabetes by the time it ends!" Carter's injection of humour had worked and he knew by Martin's response a little of the tension, just for now, had been alleviated.

Jack had taken longer to recover from the savagery of the killing at the public toilets than the two killings before. His body had been ravaged by the compelling insanity driving him and the sheer ferocity with which he had undertaken the murder had exhausted him. He was now ready however to up the stakes in the game of cat and mouse he was playing with the police. Jack was planning something, something very special. His cunning was as unnerving as his madness.

Jack left Compton Street the next morning. He was clutching a large brown -coloured, heavily padded packet. He strode with purpose down the road, crossing the carriageways with more care now, he had been in the city a while and was much more accustomed to the heavy volume of traffic found there. As he walked down North Street he gathered increasing momentum. It was another cold brisk day and Brighton's North Street was just as busy as ever. Jack heard several people as he walked by them, discussing the series of brutal murders in the town and his stature seemed to physically grow as he almost fed off the energy of the fear in their voices.

Before too long Jack reached the town hall buildings situated adjacent to the Brighton Lanes, which were only a short distance away from Compton Street. Once there he walked directly up to the front of the large impressive building. The modern electric doors opened and without pausing he walked straight in. There was no queue at the long front desk. It was, in fact, unusually quiet, a very camp and smart young man behind the counter called Jack forward straight away.

"Can I help you sir?" the young man asked politely.

"This is a package for Councillor Jonathon Morgan," Jack replied, his black piercing eyes staring intently at the young man who sat behind the counter. "He is expecting it," he added. The young man dutifully put the package in the in-tray box behind him and when he turned around again the tall handsome stranger was gone. He thought no more about the matter and settled back down to his computer and carried on with his usual admin duties, totally unaware he had just seen and survived a meeting with the man who was the actual 'Brighton Ripper'.

Jack set off back up North Street. He showed scant regard for any of the people or the bustling crowds and the highly decorated shop windows he passed on his route. He had just put his catalyst for chaos and panic in the city into action and he was intent solely on waiting for the plan to unfold. He hurried back to the security of Compton Street, his nerves now jangling with excited anticipation.

Councillor Morgan had been out most of that morning. He had chaired a meeting at one of the council's remote buildings and had met several of his friends afterwards, for a quick coffee and a social catch-up. The councillor had declared his continued outrage at the killings taking place in the city and he was using the awful events cleverly to sustain his self-proclaimed appointment, as in his words, "the voice of the gay community of Brighton".

"Oh, Councillor Morgan, there is some post here for you, sir," the young man behind the counter said upon seeing his return to the building. "Yes, here we are one large parcel and a large number of letters; here they are, sir." Morgan was unsurprised by the amount of post he had received that morning. Every day he had people writing to him to express their horror at the ongoing murders and supporting his stance on the action or inaction, as he saw it, of the local police. He clutched the in tray tightly and took it with him into the lift.

"More mail then, sir?" the pretty female clerk said who shared the lift with him up to the first floor.

"Yes, I'm certainly popular at the moment," the councillor replied with a proud smile.

"Oh good, you are back, sir," Morgan's secretary said as he came through to go into his office. "Don't forget you have a press interview at three o'clock this afternoon for an update on your part in stopping these awful murders," she said.

"Yes, yes, Susan," the councillor retorted. "I'm just going to open this mail, any other messages?"

"Yes sir. Mick Thompsett rang; he wanted to know when you could go over this month's audit with him," and with that the councillor went into his office and shut the door, without so much as acknowledgement of her statement, let alone a courteous reply. She was used to the councillor's manner however having worked with him for years and it certainly didn't affront the loyal secretary.

In general, however, Councillor Morgan was not a well-liked man within the building, despite holding a responsible and senior position. He was a particularly short man, but he had a very big attitude, and what he lacked in physical stature he made up for by not being afraid to voice his often very opinionated views. He regularly and openly criticised other public servants in the community, including the local police and even the town council to which he was partially affiliated; he also cleverly manipulated his sexuality for his own ends. He did, however, yield a lot of power and influence, and enjoyed jousting with and influencing the press. His propaganda skills were polished and he did his level best to make sure he always got painted in a good light. He was, if nothing else, desperate to show a good standing in the community as an ambassador for all his constituents. The councillor also saw himself as an advocate and orator for the gay community, both as a self-appointed leader and additionally as a campaigner for equality. Most of the community, though, especially the gay community saw through his two-faced facade, however, these murders had raised his profile and more people than ever were supporting his actions, something he intended to ensure continued.

Suddenly and without any warning a man's high-pitched scream could be heard emulating from the closed office of the newly returned Councillor Morgan. Immediately his secretary ran into the office, concerned at what on earth could be wrong. As she stood in his doorway, the councillor was staggering backward trying to get some distance between himself and his large antique desk. He was ashen and grey and looked as if at any moment he was going to be violently sick. Unable to speak coherently he mumbled to his confused secretary, "We, we must get out of here." The pair hurriedly left the room, the councillor almost being held upright by the petite woman.

Once outside his office and despite feeling weak at the knees, Morgan with some urgency found the energy to forcefully slam his office door shut. "I must wash my hands," he said, as he raised two blood-stained hands toward her. She ushered him out of her room and across the corridor into the toilet opposite, assuming he had injured himself with something.

"What is it, sir?" she said pensively. "What on earth is wrong?"

The councillor was hyperventilating as he now leaned against the washroom sink. His secretary ran the taps on the sink to assist him in being able to wash his hands. As he scrubbed them clean he looked her in the eyes. "My mail," he said. "There is a body part, in my mail!"

By now all the offices on the same floor, and even some from the ground floor, had people buzzing around eager to find what and who exactly had been the source of the piercing scream. Imba Justin, Morgan's right-hand man and based in the office next door to Morgan had been one of the first in the corridor. He had established quickly the councillor had received something awful in the mail. He also had managed to ascertain that there was nothing that would contaminate or endanger anyone else in the building and soon started to reassure everyone, telling them there was nothing for them to worry about. Imba placated their interest, by stating quite correctly, that the councillor had just had an awful shock and the best thing they could do despite their concerns, was to go back to their own offices and get on with their work.

Councillor Morgan had come out of the toilet by this time and was now perched awkwardly on the edge of a nearby chair, still shaking violently, and still in the company of his secretary. The diligent and caring woman had not left the councillor's side. Slowly, everyone started to disperse and soon there was only Imba Justin, his colleague Michael Afflick, who shared his office, and Morgan's secretary who were still all left in the room.

"Now calmly, Jon, what was actually in the package?" Justin asked tentatively.

"It's a… a body part I think," Morgan said. "I think we should call the police," he added.

"Yes," said his secretary and she got up and walked with purpose towards the phone.

"No!" Justin shouted abruptly and then lowered his voice again. "No, don't call them yet, let me check first in the office, we don't want to make a mistake and humiliate the councillor."

Justin left the others and with much trepidation went into Morgan's office. Morgan, in his panic, had dropped the newly opened package and the item contained within, which Justin could see, was wrapped in a handkerchief. The handkerchief was saturated in dry but tarry, coagulated, black blood with the body part inside it clearly visible. Being dropped so violently had caused it to protrude from its material wrapping. Justin could see even though it was ripped and mangled, that it was clearly a penis and it looked as if it had testicles still attached to it. He also saw a piece of bloodied paper that had fallen from the package it had arrived in, and he poked at the paper tentatively with a pen from the top of Morgan's desk and flipped it over to see what was written on it. Justin studied the paper carefully and although it was difficult to see easily because it was half-folded and blood- stained, it looked like there were four lines of writing on it. He had read all the reports in the papers, some had suggested, although the police had not confirmed it, that the so-called 'Brighton Ripper' always left a four-line poem at the scene of his awful crimes. Justin was putting two and two together. This is direct from the 'Brighton Ripper' himself he thought, his nerves jangling. Before leaving the office again Justin took a deep, large breath and stood by the door for a moment to compose his feelings, before going back out to the councillor.

He reappeared from the office and he said calmly to Morgan's secretary as if totally unperturbed. "Do not call the police, Susan, not yet. I'm not sure they are needed. But be a dear could you? Go and find me a plastic bag, oh, ideally not a clear one, and a pair of cleaning gloves."

"What are you bloody doing, Imba?" Morgan said. He was still shaking and traumatised and by this point was sipping erratically from a cup of water he had been given, trying to compose himself.

"Come into my office for a moment, Jon," Justin said. "And you, Michael," he added. Justin shut the door once the three men were safely inside. He took a deep breath in and out once more and quietly said, "I know you are still in shock, Jon, but you are right that is a body part in your office."

"Oh my God," Morgan said.

"But more than that I'm sure it's a body part that has been sent directly to you from the 'Brighton Ripper'," Justin added.

"Fucking hell," Afflick said. "Then we must call the police surely, Imba."

"No, no, wait. Think, Jon," Justin went on. "This is your chance to humiliate Martin and the police. Can't you see, you are the victim here Jon, the victim! Imagine the publicity. We cannot miss this opportunity, it's perfect, perfect."

Imba Justin was a very clever man. In fact, all of the three men present had gone to university together. They were also all very politically active and very good friends. Morgan was astute and had surrounded himself, at least in the immediate offices around his own, with people he could trust and rely on for support. The three men were also homosexual and had attended many campaigning rallies together bringing to the fore injustices, as they saw them, in their formative years. They all disliked the police and thought that many officers were homophobic, a belief established after clashes at these demonstrations and their numerous subsequent arrests. Justin knew this was a chance for them as a group of like-minded campaigners, to slap the police in the face, as well as raise his boss's political profile and gain sympathy from the public for being targeted by such a maniac as the 'Brighton Ripper'.

Morgan was starting to come around to Justin's way of thinking and Afflick, too, now he had evaluated the situation, agreed on this course of action. "Michael," Justin said. "Can you go and call the press office? Yes, tell them Councillor Morgan wishes to rearrange the press interview for later this afternoon. Tell them he now has some breaking news to disclose and he wants the interview held outside the John Street police station at four o'clock. That will give us enough time to prepare a speech for you, Jon, and allow us to make some placards and billboards. Yes, Jon, then we will gather as many people as we can here and you will march to the John Street police station and at the press conference reveal your horror, indignation and fear at receiving such a distressing package through the post. Something of course your local police failed to prevent. It will make you, Jon, it will make you," Justin said excitedly.

In the world of politics it is well known to get on you must raise your profile. Justin had no intent to do anything unlawful he was just raising the profile and standing of his boss within the community, something he was paid to do.

Jack had engineered this whole situation perfectly; he did not know it just yet, but soon there would be chaos. The kind of chaos that would do exactly what he wanted, assist in his evading capture. That was his top priority, the fear and other ensuing complications for his adversaries and the public at large were just a welcomed bonus.

CHAPTER FOURTEEN

Back at the John Street police station, Martin had no idea what events were unfolding in the town hall. He and his hard-working team of dedicated detectives were already busy trying to cope with an increasing number of calls and reports about the horrific killings. Although some were cranks and people who were trying to ascertain some status through the notoriety of false confessions, much of the information sent in was genuine and orchestrated by people who honestly thought they had seen something out of the ordinary and who were motivated only by trying to help. The problem for Martin and his police team was how to separate the good information from the bad. Martin knew someone out there knew something or had most likely seen, or even met and spoken to the killer, and just not known it and how right he was.

"Ah, Susan the bag and the gloves, thank you," Justin said. He had come out of his office and left the other two men, Afflick and Morgan, actively discussing his proposal.

"I still think we should tell the police what has happened," Morgan's secretary said.

"Oh, didn't I tell you, Susan? We are going to, yes it's all in hand, we are going to let the police know exactly what has happened here today," Justin added and he went back into Morgan's office pulling on the gloves the confused and shaken secretary had just got for him. Once inside Morgan's office, Justin composed himself again. He moved towards the desk and carefully knelt on the ground next to the handkerchief, with its awful content clearly visible. With trembling hands and his heart almost beating through his chest, he picked up the handkerchief with the exposed genitals captured inside. He gulped and swallowed hard as he put it quickly into the ribbed white plastic bag Morgan's diligent secretary had found for him. He then placed that bag into a large brown envelope he took out from one of Morgan's well-stocked desk drawers. This completed, he turned his attention to the ripped-open brown original packet and the folded piece of bloodied paper that had fallen beside it. He placed the packaging in the envelope and picked up the half-folded note. He unfolded the paper and with both his hands shaking, he lifted it up to read what it said. He smiled self-satisfyingly as he saw it was indeed a verse of four lines. He read it in an almost excited but terrified whisper quietly to himself. It read:

> "Thy manhood so your loin does grace,
>
> Removed twill look so out of place,
>
> In time, one ripper will ever you see,
>
> Now write my place in your history."

Justin gulped again, swallowing hard once more and then placed this piece of paper too into the envelope. He took a final deep breath, stood up and walked out of the room. "Right," he said putting on a brave face for the sole benefit of Morgan's secretary. "Now we must get on with calling the police," he said as he walked past where she sat; he left the room and went back into the corridor and into his own office. He shut the door of his office and blowing out a breath he said excitedly, but with more than just a hint of further trepidation, "It's in here." He looked at Morgan and Afflick who were both staring unbelievingly at him.

"Well, just put it on the bloody desk then," Morgan said still terrified.

"Listen, Jon," Justin said. "You are going to have to hold that envelope. I'll get us all a coffee and then I'll tell you about the poem inside it. It must be as I thought from the 'Brighton Ripper' himself. You are going to have to know what is written on the paper in the package to be able to tell the press. It will be sensational, Jon, sensational!"

"I think you are bloody enjoying this," Michael Afflick said.

"Well," said Justin. "Let's just say every cloud has a silver lining." He laughed gently and left the room.

"Twelve sugars in my coffee please!" Morgan called loudly after him. The normally officious man was not feeling like any press interview, not just yet.

Jack was sat once again at Compton Street. He knew by now it was likely that Councillor Morgan had received his package. Jack had decided he would go back to the town hall after a few hours just to see if his plan was working. He knew he must be careful, after all the front office clerk had seen him once and might recognise him if he went too close to the town hall reception. An overwhelming excitement was exuding from Jack and he gave a small uncontrolled tremor. He oozed an aura of almost tangible confidence and was sure his plan would incite the mayhem he so desperately hoped to have engineered. He sat back in the armchair, rested and waited, although he was hardly able to contain himself. "Not too much longer, not too much longer, Jack," he muttered madly under his breath.

The time at the town hall was going so very quickly. Justin and Afflick had arranged for the press conference to be upgraded and it was to be situated outside the front office reception of the John Street police station itself. Morgan was practising holding the envelope without shaking and he had been briefed by Justin on its content and the verse that was within it. Morgan was a clever man and retained information clearly and could recall it exactly. His confidence was growing and his ego was being stroked by the anticipation of all the attention, he knew that he would shortly be receiving.

By now a small crowd was gathering outside the town hall. Word was spreading in the community that there was to be a protest march led by Councillor Morgan himself, to express the need for more police action, given the recent spate of dreadful killings. Things were going well, and Justin and Afflick were tingling with an instinctive nervous energy at the prospects of the drama to come.

Back at the John Street police station word was filtering through from beat officers and members of the public that there was to be a march led by Councillor Morgan that afternoon to display his outrage, and that of the community as a whole, that police seemed powerless to stop the evil and horrendous killings in the town.

"Have you heard the news, governor?" Carter said to his boss. "Morgan's organised a march up here to 'the nick' now; some sort of a protest I have been told."

"God," Martin said. "Does Morgan not bloody know how that will stir things up; what the hell is he playing at? We are overstretched for manpower as it is."

"Yes, governor, and already the press are gathering at the front of 'the nick'," Carter said. "There are even television reporters and everything. It's already unmitigated chaos out there, sir."

"Right, John, in that case, will you ask the uniformed duty inspector to put some of his officers out there to keep things calm? We don't want a bloody riot particularly not right outside 'the nick'. Get him to send a couple of uniformed officers to the town hall as well. Only a couple, though, we need to keep a low profile; we do not want to aggravate an already volatile situation. Morgan needs no encouragement or help to cause us lots of bother. I think we are better off in here, we have enough to do as it is."

Martin paused thoughtfully for a moment. "I wonder? What is Morgan up to and why this afternoon?" he said pensively. Martin was concerned but had no idea of the councillor's hidden agenda.

Still, the crowd grew in numbers outside the town hall and the three men who had planned this little escapade were feeling a frisson of excitement at the thought of the forthcoming events. Their earlier terror and shock at the morning's postal delivery were being suppressed by this gut-tingling anticipation and the tension in the air was palpable. All the majority of the hard-working staff in the rest of the town hall building knew was that the officious Councillor Morgan had received a letter of some sort that had enraged him and forced him into the action of organising a march and a press conference at the John Street police station. Most knew Morgan and the fact he would not pass up the opportunity to raise his profile in the community given the chance, so this sudden choice of action had not surprised them. He was a man who did nothing by halves.

"It's time, Jon," Justin said to Morgan. The councillor had changed his clothing and put on his best suit that was always kept pressed and ready at his office and by now he was so full of adrenaline that holding and carrying the envelope with its devastating content no longer fazed him. The three men got to the front glass doors of the town hall. There was a large madding crowd gathered and much muttering and murmuring going on. Those few more militant agitators Justin had organised with placards were raising the tension and anticipation of the throng and there was an air of hostility and also an underlying sense of frustration that rippled through the gathered crowd.

"Deep breath, Jon, here we go," Justin said, as Afflick went to the large glass doors to open them. Afflick then pressed a mushroom-domed green button next to the double doors which took the lock off the automatic opening facility and Morgan stepped forward and went out to greet his public. Suddenly, and quite spontaneously, there was a ripple of applause. Morgan's face glowed with pride and arrogance; he had not dreamt of such a rapturous welcome. Justin who had brought a small loudhailer out with him handed it to Morgan. Lifting it to his mouth, "I'd like to thank you all for coming," the haughty councillor said. "I cannot reveal exactly why we are marching today as yet. But suffice to say it is primarily to show the police and the people of the city that we are in unity, in the fight against the terrible killer we have living amongst us." Morgan paused for a moment, took a deep breath and puffed out his little chest he then shouted, "Are you with me?" He was being swept along by the baying crowd who were heeding and hanging on to his every last word. The thrilling experience of having such a large group focused on him was exhilarating for the pompous little man.

"Yes, we are with you!" the crowd responded in a ramshackle and disjointed reply.

"Right," Morgan said, the hairs on the back of his neck tingling. "Let us march to the John Street police station."

Jack had left the security of Compton Street he could no longer resist the driving urge to go to see what was happening at the town hall. He walked in his usual brisk fashion and was soon heading away from Compton Street and down the bustling North Street. As he got nearer to the bottom end of the road, he saw a large procession of people being led by the short, stout framed, Councillor Morgan. They had all just appeared from near the North Lanes Square. Jack's body tingled, and he gave a small violent shudder, as he read a placard that had a slogan written in red, gory, trailed paint. It said: "No More Killings. Protect Us Now. Police Take Action." He knew his plan had worked, perhaps even better than he had anticipated, and he walked more quickly to get caught up with the group and in an ever-increasing gathering of protestors, he joined the march. The 'Brighton Ripper', unbeknown to anyone present, was marching to demonstrate against his own heinous crimes and was with a crowd baying for his very capture. His anonymity and the irony of the situation excited Jack to the point of trembling.

The crowd marched through the Old Steine, now gathering momentum. The only police presence was just two uniformed town centre beat officers. These two officers were desperately trying to control the large volume of traffic, which was being brought to a standstill, without interfering with the march in any way. One constable radioed ahead to warn the police station communications room and the station's commanding officers of the coming mass of demonstrators. Cars continually tooted their horns at the large crowd as they meandered through the streets. This horn sounding was not in anger at the crowd blocking the road, but to show support and solidarity for the demonstration. The few well-chosen agitators in the group were constantly whipping up the tension of the masses and the atmosphere was literally at fever pitch. The protestors' throng collected people en route like a swarming of ants, the colony marching onward, with local people finally feeling that they were expressing their pent-up frustrations, fear and venom, constructively. And all the while, Jack marched quietly with them. He could hardly contain himself in his anticipation and wondering of what chaos was yet to come.

Outside of the John Street police station, there was a large group of press reporters gathered who were standing in the carriageway of John Street itself. The road had been coned and blocked off previously by police at both ends. A carefully structured fenced-off cordon had been formed by police. This was to give the press and reporters a separate and safe place to stand in anticipation of the large crowd expected and indeed en- route. The march and all the needs for the safety of the press and the public were creating extra stress for the uniformed duty inspector. He had, at the order of the station commander, used officers from the traffic division and the town centre patrol teams to boost the police presence outside of their city headquarters.

"Here they come now," one of the press reporters shouted and the chant of, "What do we want? Police taking action!" grew progressively louder. Morgan came into view at the head of the group. The little man's chest was puffed out and his short legs hammered into the ground, as he marched like a tyrannical leader about to go to war. Morgan looked up to the first-floor C.I.D. windows at the front of the police station. He was hoping to see Martin behind the glass watching him leading his procession of malice. Cameras flashed frantically as the press pushed police officers and one another, jostling to get the best and most prominent photographs of the militant group. In addition to the press and their photographers, there were also several television cameras recording the sequence of events. It was an extravaganza for the media and a police nightmare.

All of this unfolding action was being watched by some of the detectives from the C.I.D. offices, whose windows looked out onto John Street itself.

"Bloody look at them," Carter said. "My God, there is bloody a throng of them."

Martin stayed away from the windows; the last thing he wanted was to show Morgan he was interested in what he thought rightly was a massive publicity stunt to raise the councillor's profile. "Come away from the windows," Martin said. "Let the councillor have his glory moment; we have got a killer to catch!"

By now the marchers were gathered right outside of the John Street police station itself. They were noisy, but not violent. Most of the people on the march had only joined it just to express their concerns and abhorrence of the murders. It was not going to be a riot, just a large show of strength. Indeed, only Morgan,

Justin and Afflick knew at this time just what was yet to come. Hidden amongst the crowd, and now drifted right the way to the back and not too close to any police officers was Jack. He remained brazen enough to watch what was going to unfold and it thrilled him with an excitement, comparable to actually killing.

Morgan was now standing on top of the small brick wall which runs around the front of the John Street police station. The wall was only about two feet high and wide enough to be a secure and safe podium from which Morgan intended to address both his adoring public and the mass of waiting press. Justin was as organised as ever and handed his boss a microphone, which had been provided to him by a member of the gathered press.

"Well, firstly," Morgan said. "I am overwhelmed, but not surprised by the support and the sincerity of all of those who have marched here with me today. Whilst I know many of you may be thinking this protest march is political and to raise my own profile, you are wrong. Our homosexual community and indeed the whole community of the city of Brighton, we all know terrifyingly at this time, is I am saddened to say, under attack from a maniac killer. And now I, too, have been a victim of that maniac killer's vengeance."

There was a stunned silence amongst the crowd. Morgan for all his arrogance was an excellent orator. "Yes," Morgan went on. "Today in my mail I have received this package, the content of which is too horrific to reveal to you in its physical form. For it is, I am devastated and horrified to reveal, a body part cut from one of the 'Brighton Ripper's' victims."

A gasp went out from the crowd. Morgan lifted the envelope with the genitals inside as the cameras flashed and clicked madly again. "This act has not only sickened me," Morgan went on. "It has affronted and affected me deeply as you can imagine. But I felt it my civic duty not to just call the police and have them come to my office and whisk the item away. No, I felt it my duty to be strong, gather my trembling, wrecked self and bring it here, with you on this march today and demand the police take action to catch this monster and catch him now."

The stunned crowd was baying and becoming more aggressive in their heckling and shouting of demands. The agitators in the crowd were working them all up and inciting their more expressive verbalization. This latest revelation by Morgan had angered and shocked everyone present, exactly as it was intended to do. The crowd continued chanting together and were calling Morgan's name and he had to raise his voice once again to be heard over them. "I would ask," he said. "No, I would insist, he went on, the officer in charge of the investigation Detective Chief Inspector Tim Martin to come down here, and with you all as witnesses, take this horrendous and shocking piece of evidence and act on it."

The uniformed sergeant stood by the door of the police station, and in seeing and hearing what was happening turned frantically to a young police constable standing next to him. "Get Martin quick," he said. "Ask him to come out here now, or there will be a bloody riot." The young constable dashed into the station.

"Whilst we are waiting for the detective chief inspector," Morgan added. "Can I ask you for some silence, for inside this terrible package there was a poem and just to prove to you all gathered here today that it is from the so-called fiend the 'Brighton Ripper'

I will read its awful content to you." Justin and Afflick were thrilled with the way the whole event was unfolding; by this point in the demonstration, you could have cut the atmosphere with a knife. Jack was watching the events unfold and had himself an intensity of glee, although he had slipped further and further back through the crowd. He knew Martin would be out shortly and though confident he was fairly safe, his instinct, the thing that helped him from getting caught, nagged at him to keep a distance away from the police detective chief inspector. The crowd hushed. Morgan said. "The poem reads thus:

> Thy manhood so your loin does grace,
> Removed twill look so out of place,
> In time, one ripper will ever you see,
> Now write my place in your history."

The crowd gasped and a huge chattering of discontent spread like a virus amongst the gathered assembly. Morgan had only read the poem in truth to shock the public and the press. It clearly identified the body part that he had been sent and he knew in its absolute depravity would aid the profile he had engineered, that of being another victim of the so-called 'Brighton Ripper'. Morgan went on now in full flow. "Mentally, I am as you can imagine," he said, "traumatised by…"

Martin came out of the police station. His blood was boiling, he knew exactly what Morgan was doing and he was angry, frustrated and hurt. His professionalism meant he knew he must conduct his response with poise and dignity and not show any anger. But inside his gut was clenched.

"Ah, Detective Chief Inspector," Morgan said. "As

I am sure you have heard, tragically I now too have been victimised by this murderer that walks freely amongst us in our city. Here I have to pass on to you, with my shock and abhorrence, the ghoulish package I was sent. I would like you to know I and everyone else in this city expect action. We need this killer caught and caught now!"

"Have you any reply, inspector?" one of the reporters called as the cameras flicked and flashed frantically again.

Martin spoke calmly but firmly. "I can assure the councillor and every member of this city we have been, will be and are doing everything in our power to catch this killer. I will need time to get this package checked. Beyond this I cannot comment further at this time. I will call a press conference when I have all the facts. In the meantime, I would ask people to remain calm. We are doing all we can."

Martin turned to go back into the station, and as he did so a voice from the crowd shouted. "It's not enough," and the whole group lurched forward.

Morgan appealed for calm and in seeing tensions rising further said, "No, we should let the officer do his job. Because I will keep everyone up to date with all the events. I can promise you that," he said his voice spiked with venom. "Thank you for your support. Would you please disperse quickly and safely, we are and will not be intimidated by any killer no matter how ruthless. And rest assured, your gesture here today has made a real difference in making us all more secure, in this our very own beloved City of Brighton."

Morgan was delighted with the whole fiasco; not only had he humiliated Martin, but he had, he knew, ingratiated himself to the whole community and secured lucrative media interest in himself for a long while to come. As Morgan finished this eloquent and rousing peroration Martin caught sight of two dark piercing eyes staring at him from the crowd. For a moment, he focused on the eyes. He looked twice, that's Kowalski he thought, mistaking Jack for Kowalski. Instinctively he pushed his way toward the back of the crowd.

"It appears the shock of my package and its content has made our senior officer forget which way the police station front door is," Morgan jibed. Martin continued to push his way through the large crowd. It only took him only a few seconds, but when he got there, Jack was gone. The marchers slowly dispersed chatting and gossiping amongst themselves. Martin walked back towards the police station. People in the crowd jostled him and showed him little respect, his mind, however, was elsewhere. He started to wonder if he was now seeing things. This case was getting to him even before the events of today, but by now he was fraught, unnerved and humiliated.

Jack settled back into the security of the tatty armchair he spent so much time in at his Compton Street home. He had left the crowd and made it safely back to the ramshackle abode and although wary of Martin, he had now actually looked directly into the eyes of his adversary. The experience had thrilled Jack and he had enjoyed the culmination of the day's events. He knew the media would now hound Martin relentlessly and that the plan he had hatched had made the press even more of a catalyst in the spreading of fear, chaos and uncertainty. The quest of the police to apprehend him would be even harder now. Jack was also aware there would be more vigilantes on the streets as well, but these 'Ripper' hunters he knew did not really know who or what they were looking for. Morgan had become his second patsy, not in the guise of another suspect, but just as a puppet, with Jack pulling the proverbial strings. The story and the history Jack was writing again, as surely as if he penned it himself.

"Bloody hell, governor," Carter said. "What the fuck just happened there?"

"Morgan. Morgan just railroaded us, John," Martin said.

Carter went on. "And when I came down and went outside to give you some moral support you suddenly shot off, governor. What was that all about?"

"Well, fuck knows, John? I thought I saw Kowalski staring at me from the back of the crowd and for some inexplicable reason I ran towards him. It was as if I was pulled towards him. I can't explain it," Martin said.

"And was it him?" Carter asked intrigued.

"Yes; no, I'm not sure," Martin said. "And, to be honest, if it was him, what would I have done? I mean, I can't arrest him for being at a demonstration. I just don't know; this case is getting to me, John. Anyway, he wasn't there. Let's take this package to Marshall and see if it is genuine. I badly need some fucking air."

The two men left the station and got into one of the C.I.D. pound cars. As they sat inside Carter said, "Morgan read out a poem to the press I heard."

"Yes, my old friend," Martin replied. "He did, loathe him or love him he manipulated that situation perfectly for his own end. He will be gloating when we have to go and get his statement."

"Never mind him, governor. He can do as he wants. We are here to catch a murderer. Morgan can wait, let's go and see Marshall like you said." Carter started the engine and the pair of detectives drove out of the rear of the police yard. The time was getting on and Martin and Sergeant Carter only just caught Marshall, who was getting ready to leave the morgue and go home.

"Sorry we are so late," Martin said. "Could we ask you to take a look at this?" He held up the brown envelope he was clutching.

"Yes of course," Marshall said. She could see Martin was quite desperate and had a lot on his mind. "I heard you had a few dramas at the station today?" she said.

"Bad news travels fast," Carter replied.

"Yes," she went on. "Councillor Morgan got a package of some sort I was told?"

"Yes," Martin said. "This is it and he claims inside it is a body part, a penis. So you can just imagine where my mind went straight away."

"Yes, our victim in the toilet, Tim. Maybe he is being truthful, that is just too coincidental to not be fact."

"Yes, I know and we have not looked inside the envelope. Instead, we decided to come straight here. I'm sure any evidential value, if it is the missing genitals, is gone, but just in case, we didn't want to examine it without you there."

"No, of course not," Marshall replied. "Just give me a minute. I'll get a gown on and we can examine it together." Marshall took the package from Martin and emptied the contents from it onto a shiny, silver dissecting table. "Right," she said. "Firstly, there is a handkerchief which has been saturated with blood. Oh yes and here," she said, carefully pulling the handkerchief away with a pair of sterile forceps from the object inside. "Here is a penis and testicles."

"My God," Carter said. "Do you think?"

But before he could finish his sentence, Marshall said. "Yes, John, most likely, it is definitely of human origin." Marshall knew the sergeant was going to ask if it could be the missing genitals from the last victim. "I will need to confirm it with tissue samples from the corpse," she went on. "But, I think we will discover that the genitals came from our victim. And on the handkerchief, gentleman, beyond the bloodstain, there is a black embroidered letter 'J'. For Jack perhaps I'm guessing if this is our murderer's alter ego?" Marshall said enquiringly.

"Or Jacub, our chief suspect," Carter said.

"Oh, God knows," Martin said. "I'm just not sure anymore."

"Anyway," Marshall went on. "Look, there is another note here. I know you probably know what it says but let's open it. I would like to read it as its format and writing style will confirm if this package was handled and sent by our killer." Marshall opened the note. "It is another quatrain," she said, "and the handwriting is the same." she read it out loud:

> "Thy manhood so your loin does grace,
>
> Removed twill look so out of place,
>
> In time, one ripper will ever you see,
>
> Now write my place in your history."

"Okay," Martin said. "So it's him. We at least know that. Mary can you give the envelope and all its content the works? Anything we can get from it will be useful. I suspect, as I already said to you, Morgan and his staff have contaminated the evidential value of it. With some hope, there will be some fingerprint evidence on the package, but with the guise of this killer I very much doubt they will be his."

"Yes, I agree, Tim," Marshall replied.

"We must be sure, however. We will get the prints off anyone who has touched the package and if you can find any fibres or anything useful, can you let us know as soon as possible? Oh yes, and can you confirm in writing that the genitals came from our victim."

"Yes, of course, Tim. I'll stay on here and get that done and send you the report over for the morning."

"Thanks, Mary," Martin said. "Right, John, let's go and debrief the troops and go home; it's been a bloody terrible day again."

That evenings de-brief was not prolonged. It was already time for the detectives to go off duty when Martin and Carter got back to the police station. Most of the press posted outside the front of John Street had scuttled off to write lengthy and sensational revelations of the day's events. The two detectives would not be harassed by reporters in the backyard of the building in any event. Since the escalation of the case, Martin had ensured, to keep reporters from bothering both himself and his officers, that there was a uniformed constable patrolling the entrance to it at all times.

By now all of the detectives knew the surprising chain of the late afternoon's events. 'The nick' was a place where news, especially bad news, spread quickly. The game of Chinese whispers was afoot, but everyone was tired and rumours distorted facts so Martin called all the detectives together and was concise and to the point. "Most, or probably all of you, now know the events of this afternoon," he said.

"Councillor Morgan was sent a package containing genitals, which we will confirm overnight, but were probably the sex organs missing from our last victim. The media and press hype will be unprecedented. So please, please, I implore you do not get drawn into any supposition or give any information to anyone, even to friends and family outside of this police station. I value you all, we work hard and play hard. We will catch this bastard, everyone. Let's all make sure we bloody well do. It's a new day tomorrow; see you all sharp in the morning at seven a.m."

He turned to John Carter, "I'm going to mine for a quiet drink. I'm not going to risk going to the pub and being seen by reporters. Do you want to come back for a quick drink, John, and perhaps we can put our heads together and see where the fuck we go from here?"

"Yes, governor, of course," Carter said. Even though he was tired he was as keen as Martin to capture this devious killer. As much as their sanity and professionalism demanded their emotional detachment, this case had become personal for both men. "I'll get my coat," Carter said quietly.

CHAPTER FIFTEEN

The next morning everyone assembled as usual for the seven o'clock briefing. The detective chief inspector came into the major incident room, which was packed with all the extra detectives the case seemed to demand, as its complexity had escalated. A ripple of voices went around the room, which smelt strongly of morning coffee and was punctuated by detectives with greying and bloodshot eyes, both from a lack of sleep and constant duress.

"Okay, settle down, everyone," Sergeant Carter said.

Martin took the lead. "Following yesterday's fiasco with Councillor Morgan, I have had the full report on the content of the package he left us with back from Marshall and forensics," he said. "She has confirmed, as we all thought, through tissue sampling that the genitals sent to the councillor are indeed those of our third victim Marcus Robertson." Another ripple went around the room. "There were two sets of fingerprints found on the package that the councillor received and although I have not confirmed this, one set is likely to be Councillor Morgan's and the other whoever the package was handed to. That does tell us something important, however. This lack of multiple prints on our package suggests that our killer delivered this envelope to the town hall himself. Had it been delivered by courier or even by another member of the public, there would have been more than two sets of prints on it.

Sergeant Carter, myself and you, D.C. Thompson, will be going to the town hall first thing this morning to take statements and get fingerprints from Councillor Morgan and whoever took the package in. It is just possible that there may be C.C.T.V. footage of our killer delivering the package itself." Another ripple of agreement and muted excitement trickled around the room. "With that in mind, I want everyone back here for a one-off briefing at noon lunchtime today, to review any new evidence disclosed to us at the town hall this morning. Okay, people, you are working hard but we still need to follow up all those other leads; let's get this done."

Martin's morning briefing was not as regimented or orderly as normal. This was quite deliberate, the whole team's morale was now completely at rock bottom. Overnight the press and media had enjoyed a field day on the story and Martin knew it was his job to rally his team and raise their spirits. He was feeling the strain himself, so he knew they all must be too. He turned to D.C. Dave Smith, "Dave, you are doing a great job with collations but follow up on that camera again from the Duke's Mound killing would you please? That could be such a significant piece of evidence. Right, everyone, let's get to it, see you all back here at twelve, hopefully with some good news for us all. Right, John," he said. "That's the three of us off. You can drive Thompson," he added, throwing the keys to the detective constable. "John, I've arranged for one of the scenes of crime officers to meet us at the town hall. He or she can check, just in case there is anything in the offices that is worth dusting and also, I'll get them to take Morgan's prints and the front counter assistant who must have taken the package. S.O.C.O.; officers take fingerprints so much better than us, John," Martin said and laughed. "Right, that's us set. Let's go."

Martin, Carter and D.C. Thompson arrived at the town hall. It was just after half past eight in the morning. Martin knew Morgan always got in to work early, the councillor was always keen to get in and organise his day. The three detectives were let into reception by the building's caretaker who told them that Councillor Morgan was already in his office.

"Ah," Morgan said as the three police officers went into the room. "A trio of detectives, finally taking the case seriously are you?" he retorted. Martin ignored the comment.

"We need you to give us a statement, councillor, please," Martin said. "And we will need a statement from whoever else touched the package that you received. We have found two sets of prints on it and they both will need to be eliminated as those from any potential suspect."

"Oh, they will be mine and Jason's," Morgan said. "Jason is the new boy in our office reception; he told me the package was there and handed it to me when I came back from my meeting. He will be in the admin offices downstairs. Be gentle with him," Morgan said sarcastically.

"Okay, John," Martin said to his sergeant. "You take a statement from Mr Morgan and I'll go downstairs and see the receptionist lad with D.C. Thompson. Do you have C.C.T.V. monitoring here as well?" Martin asked the grinning Morgan.

"Oh yes, actually we do." Morgan's eyes flickered for a moment; he could have kicked himself for not thinking of that before. "Yes and the tapes," he said and added untruthfully. "I had already thought you would want to see them; they will all be in the admin office as well."

As Martin and D.C. Thompson went back downstairs they crossed the caretaker going up the stairs to the first floor. "Mr. Martin," the caretaker said, "the scenes of crime officer. She is in reception."

"Oh thanks," Martin said. "Can you tell us if we can get access straight into the admin offices?"

"Oh yes," the caretaker said. "Who do you want to see?"

"A Jason," Martin answered.

"Oh young Jason Pierre, yes he will be in there now. Just go around the front desk. The door to the administration room is at the far end of it, you will see it and it stays open; they will not close it until we open the foyer to the general public," he added.

"Oh hello, sir, that has saved me coming to look for you," the heavily tattooed female scenes of crime officer said to Martin as he and D.C. Thompson got to the bottom of the stairs. "What shall I do first, sir?"

Martin thought for a brief minute. "Can you go up and get Councillor Morgan's fingerprints and then come back down here? We have got a lad we are talking to down in reception, Jason Pierre. We will be getting a statement from him, and he will need his prints to be taken, too. Yes and by then, we should know if there is anything else here you should be examining for us."

"Okay, sir," she said. "That's fine."

Martin and Thompson went through and into the admin office. "Jason Pierre?" Martin said enquiringly as he and D.C. Thompson went into the brightly painted room.

"Yes, that's me," a tall skinny young lad said in a camp high-pitched retort. "I'm Jason Pierre, are you from the police?"

"Yes," said Martin. "My officer here is going to take a statement from you and we will need you to have your fingerprints taken, too, but before all that, you took the package for Councillor Morgan, didn't you, young man?"

"Oh, how exciting," the young man almost squealed. "Yes, sir, I did. Goodness if only I had known I would not have touched it. I said to my mum, I was horrified. I mean it is not every day in this office you get a penis in a parcel. Shocking," he said. "Shocking it was!"

"Yes, I'm sure," Martin said. "That said, I am sure you may now realise the significance of seeing the man who delivered it. Can you describe him to us, the person who gave the package to you?"

"Oh, my goodness," the young man squealed again. "You think don't you, oh you think he was. He was the 'Brighton Ripper'? Oh my days, get me a chair, oh, my days," he said brimming with excitement. "Wait until I tell my mum she will be so shocked."

"Mr Pierre," Martin said trying to calm the excitable young man down but not to worry him. "We are not sure who the person was who gave you the package, but if, and I mean it is only an if at this time, if this was indeed our suspect your best choice is to tell us and us only. This man is dangerous."

Suddenly the young receptionist realised the serious nature of the events he had witnessed. "Yes," he said. "Oh, will he come after me? Oh, my days. Oh dear. Oh dear!"

"No," Martin said. "I don't think for one minute he will, even if it was the killer. What is important is that you give us his description as accurately as you can."

"He, well yes, let me think," the flustered young

man replied, all his earlier excitement had now turned to anxiety. He knew this was no longer a game, this was serious. "I will tell you all I know," he added.

"Okay, just wait one minute," Martin said, as the young man seemed on the verge of blurting out his description, such was his nervous anxiety. Martin turned to D.C. Thompson. "Dave," he said. "Get your notebook and just jot this description down will you please? Yes go ahead, Jason."

"Well, he was about thirty, although I'm not that good with age. Well, I look so young myself you see, I moisturise every night you know."

Martin sighed, he knew this interview was going to be difficult, but it was vital to the investigation, so he persevered with the questioning. "Okay, so he was aged about thirty, fine, please carry on."

"Well, to be honest," Mr Pierre said. "To be honest, I would describe him as tall, dark and handsome. Yes, that was him: tall, dark and handsome."

Martin could see the young man trying to recall the man's features. "How tall exactly?" Martin asked.

"Oh, about six feet, oh yes, and he had lovely dark wavy hair, oh yes, and his eyes, piercing they were, black I think, yes black. Yes, I noticed his eyes; they were as black as coal."

"And what about his skin colour?" Martin asked.

"Oh yes, white, yes, definitely white. But foreign looking too, if you know what I mean."

"You said foreign looking? What exactly do you mean?" Martin was excited by the young man's description. Thus far, he had described the young student Doctor Kowalski. Martin now thought with some certainty, that Kowalski was either the killer he sought or at the very least involved in the killings in some way. "Foreign looking?" he said to the young man again, Martin's voice hung on the question.

"Well, he had a sort of foreign mannerism; it's hard to describe, a look about him an aura."

"Okay," Martin wanted to clarify the point. "Did he have a foreign accent of any kind?"

"I don't remember," the young man replied. "I can't recall. He barely spoke to me, one brief sentence, he was, I am a little unsure, I think quietly spoken, but quite curt, yes, quite curt when he spoke."

Martin was a little disappointed; an accent of any kind made suspects easier to identify. He moved the questioning along. "What about facial features?" Martin asked. "Apart from his eyes, did he have a moustache or a beard or big ears or anything to distinguish him by?"

"Oh, I'm not sure," the young man said. "Oh, I just don't remember my head is spinning now."

"Take your time, you are doing really well," Martin said, gently encouraging his young witness on this vital point.

"Yes, he was, I remember, clean-shaven I think. Yes, clean-shaven. Oh, and very smart and clean. I notice those things you know," the receptionist said smiling. The young man was relaxing a little again. "Oh, and he smelt nice, too. We don't get a lot of young men in here who smell nice," he added and laughed. He continued: "He smelt sort of clinically clean, you know, just like you'd expect a doctor to smell like; yes, he had that about him, too. If I hadn't known better, I'd have guessed he was a doctor."

The receptionist had stopped Martin in his tracks. The young man mentioning the word 'doctor' had shocked and delighted Martin, even though it was a supposition.

The receptionist was quite astute and a witness could often without even realising it, when they had met a killer, form a perception of their character which sometimes could be worth exploring further. This man has seen Kowalski, Martin thought again to himself. It must be him, it must be. Martin paused trying to retain his own, now overexcited, emotions.

"Okay and one more thing before you give your full statement to my detective. Please think very carefully before you answer this, it is important," Martin said, his voice quivering; this was vital, and he knew it. "Do you think you could recognise this man if you were to see him again?"

The young man now paused. "Yes, I think so. Oh I am not sure. I only saw him so briefly, maybe because of his dark eyes, but in what way? Like an identity parade? Like on television?" the young man asked.

"Yes like that," Martin said.

"Well yes, I could try, I think, well I could try," the young man answered. The certainty in his recollection of the man was diminishing. "I'd hate to pick out the wrong person, though, and I'm not sure. I'm not sure," he said.

Martin's heart sank a little. He knew this was vital to the case and if he called an identity parade, then this time he had to be sure Kowalski would be recognised. To date, this young man was the only eyewitness still living who may have seen the young student doctor if that was who the man in the town hall had been. But all was not lost for Martin he still had the C.C.T.V. footage. If Kowalski appeared on that Martin knew he could use the young receptionist's description to corroborate the video evidence. His mind was spinning. "Well," Martin said, "with luck, young man," seeing he had unnerved the youngster again. "He will be on your C.C.T.V. here won't he, and then we can both be certain of what he looked like, can't we?" Martin used his phrase exactingly to give more confidence to the young man's involvement. "You do have C.C.T.V. here, don't you?"

Suddenly, Martin had the terrible thought that maybe there was no C.C.T.V. in the foyer despite Morgan having already mentioned there was. Nothing after all was going smoothly in this case. To Martin's relief, the young man said. "Oh yes, and I can get you the tapes."

"Great," Martin replied, "so could you get me the tapes first and then my detective will take your full statement; oh, and if you would consent to your fingerprints being taken."

"Oh yes, of course, how exciting," the young man said. "This case is all over the papers and television. Wait till I tell my mum," he said. He had completely forgotten Martin's earlier warning.

"Yes," Martin said, he smiled despairingly. "Okay, Dave, can you get the statement please? I am going to see how Sergeant Carter is getting on."

Martin hurried up the stairs. His stomach was knotted with tension. The C.C.T.V. footage was vital to the case. He passed the scene of crime officer as he neared the landing of the stairway. "Jason Pierre," he said catching his breath. "In the admin office behind the front desk, full prints please," he added. Martin put his head around Morgan's office door. "Can I grab you for five minutes, Sergeant Carter?"

"Oh, anything I should know about?" Morgan said enquiringly.

"No, it's just a police matter," Martin said abruptly

but quietly. Carter went into the corridor and shut the office door. The two detectives stood in the corridor alone. "The young lad on reception," Martin said. "He has just given me a description of the man with the package, and he has described Kowalski."

"Bloody hell," Carter said.

"Yes, John, and they have C.C.T.V. in the foyer," Martin added. "Finish your statement, John. I'll get the tapes. We will leave Dave here to finish up. We need to get back to 'the nick' to see those tapes. If Kowalski is on them, we've got him, my old friend. We've got him, John!" he added.

The two excited detectives hurried along the corridor of the police station clutching, with great expectancy, the two foyer surveillance tapes that they had just been given at the town hall. The pair were excited in such a fashion as to be obvious to the few uniformed officers they passed in the corridors. They were in fact, more excited than they had been since the first day of this awful case.

They entered the Whisky Victor C.C.T.V. viewing suite and both pulled up a chair in front of the four viewing consuls. "Here goes," Martin said, blowing out a big breath and with his hand trembling as he put the first tape into the machine. "He's got to be on here, John," Martin said. "He has just got to be."

The two detectives played and viewed the tapes over and over again. The young receptionist could be seen, but in every shot of the tape he was alone. "It's like the railway footage, governor," Carter said despairingly. "It's as if the receptionist is talking to himself," Carter said again, now clearly exasperated.

"How can our killer not be on this tape?" Martin

exclaimed, his voice now quivering with emotion. "The package is there on the desk. Look, John. And Jason the receptionist is behind the desk and talking to someone there in front of him. There look, there. Jason picks the package up quite clearly, but all this time there is no one else in view. There is only a blank space in front of the counter. There is no one else there. Fucking hell, John, you are right. It's just like the railway station tapes. What is he? Are we hunting for a fucking ghost?"

Martin and Carter were back in Martin's office when D.C. Thompson got back to the station. The two frustrated and dejected detectives were talking as Thompson came in. "I just don't get it, John," Martin exclaimed. "I honestly expected to see Kowalski on those tapes and instead of that, nothing."

"What, nothing?" D.C. Thompson said. "Have they been wiped?"

"No, Dave, and this stays strictly in this room for now," Martin said. "The only person that can be seen on those tapes, at the times we want, is the young receptionist you just took the statement from."

"Bloody hell, sir, it's like the railway station ones I saw then." Thompson was shocked.

"Yes, I don't get it, Dave." Martin was dumbstruck.

"Well here is the receptionist's statement anyway, governor," he added, "and S.O.C.O. is liaising with Marshall to check the prints."

"Okay, Dave, get back to it son and thanks for the statement."

"I'm gutted for you, governor," he said.

"Not a word," Martin said again. "This must not get out. It will destroy morale completely and the press would have another field day," he added.

"What about the receptionist and an I.D. parade?" Carter said.

"I tested the water on that one before I saw the tapes," Martin said. "But I think it's a no-go. The young lad was dithering. He was worrying in case he picked out the wrong man. I think he is not reliable enough, especially not to put on the stand as our only key witness. Defence council would shred him, John. No, we are back to square, fucking one again."

Since the afternoon of the press conference at the John Street police station, Jack had been enjoying looking at the newspaper headlines. When he occasionally ventured from the security of Compton Street, he heard people everywhere relaying to one another their opinions and fears about both the murders and the events outside the police station. The press had gone mad for the story, and all the headlines were conveying the horror and suffering of Councillor Morgan. Morgan was appearing on television now as well as in all the papers. Jack sat content in his armchair, carefully cleaning his scalpels and everything bloodied by the brutality of his last murder. Still tingling from the thrill of his explosive catalyst, he knew it would not be long before he would excite the media further. He was going to kill again.

CHAPTER SIXTEEN

Martin was in his office by six o'clock sharp in the morning. Events over the last few days had left him reeling. John Street police station was besieged by journalists outside the front office. There was even a semi-permanent press cordon there, holding back reporters and camera crews who gathered every day. The overstretched police force had uniformed officers doing extra shifts, and Superintendent Flowers had authorised more detectives to assist Martin's team in the investigating and following up of the overwhelming numbers of calls, letters and parcels now flooding into the John Street station. They were receiving a staggering array of mail and reports, from hoax plastic body parts to letters or phone calls made or sent by people either confessing to being the by now infamous 'Brighton Ripper', or from others who were convinced they knew who the 'Ripper' now was. It was a nightmare for Martin and his team of epic proportions. This was coupled by Morgan appearing everywhere across the media platform, smearing the police investigation and protesting at his suffering at the hands of, as he called him the beastly 'Brighton Ripper'.

Martin had been summoned to attend a meeting with Superintendent Flowers, which he was to go to before the morning briefing with his detectives. The superintendent was going to organise another press conference and he was pressuring Martin to come up with something positive to tell reporters. Flowers himself was being squeezed in all directions. He had politicians getting involved in the case and casting their opinions, as well as auditors and his commanders despairing at the budget he was outlaying in this investigation with little or no results to date.

"We need some results in this case, detective chief inspector," Flowers said. "I'm getting berated by all sides. We have no choice but to call a press conference. Tell me you have something, anything!" Flower's voice was raised, not so much in anger, but in sheer desperation.

"I thought we had got him when I collected those C.C.T.V. surveillance tapes from the town hall, sir," Martin said. "But the man's a fucking ghost. I just can't seem to get any leads and there is no D.N.A. evidence. Not even fibres of anything I can trace. It's like no case I have ever known. I am chasing demons," Martin said. "I need more time, sir, I need more time!"

"Time is not a luxury we have, detective chief inspector," Flowers retorted. "It's anarchy out there, with vigilantes, the press and Morgan. We need a body and we need one now," he said.

"I know, sir," Martin replied. "Kowalski, the young student doctor fits our profile."

"But you need evidence, chief inspector!" Flowers retorted. "We are caught between a rock and a hard place. Right, we cannot go before them with nothing new. I'll stall the press conference for twenty-four hours. That's it, chief inspector, you have twenty-four hours or we are both for the high jump. And God forbid he kills again before we catch him. Right, if your gut is Kowalski, that's all we have. Twenty-four hours, follow your gut but do it the right way. You need to either establish he is completely innocent or find something to prove his guilt with certainty and with enough hard evidence to convince the C.P.S. it is him. If it is him, get him, Tim." Flower's voice softened; he knew Martin was at his wit's end. "Go with your gut, Tim," he said. "But I don't just want anyone in those cells, I want the actual killer and I want him soon!"

Martin stood before his detectives at his briefing. They all felt for him and knew the awful and considerable pressure he was under. The press, Morgan, politicians and the history of the original 'Ripper' stories were evoking passion and desperation in everyone.

"Right," Martin said. "So here we are, back here at the start again." He sighed slightly finding it hard not to show some emotion. "The only prints on our package from the town hall have been confirmed as Morgan's and the young counter clerks. The C.C.T.V. footage was no good. We can only assume whoever delivered the package was able to avoid being picked up by it. All the S.O.C.O. reports are back, and I have studied them all again first thing this morning. Apart from the red herring D.N.A. that our killer has left at the scene of every murder, there has been no other forensic evidence of any worth to date. Fingerprints at best have been partials. But there is still the possibility that these are our killers. Although, in truth, I believe he is too careful to get caught that way, he may make a mistake at some time. Especially, if God forbids, he kills again before we catch him.

The camera that was recovered from our news reporter and what seems an age ago, Dave Smith tells me, is untraceable to any store or more importantly any purchaser at this time. But I want you, Dave, to keep on following up that line of investigation. If we can find out whose camera it is, we will have another name in the frame so to speak. With no owner of the camera currently and no other quality leads, our current prime suspect is still our Doctor Jakub Kowalski. His picture is on the board here. I intend, before sending you all off this morning, to get D.C. Smith to give you all a rundown on what we know about him to date. Okay, Dave, if you would give us all you have collated from the reports thus far."

"Okay, sir. Yes, Jakub Michael Kowalski was born in Poland. Date of birth, the twenty-third of October nineteen sixty-four, he is aged twenty-four. He is from a very poor family. Tough upbringing and worked very hard to get a scholarship. He is especially talented in English, both language and literature."

"Our poet," Carter interjected. "Sorry Dave, go on," he said.

The detective constable continued: "To get him to medical school, now a student doctor, he started his career at the Royal Hospital in Whitechapel London." A ripple went around the incident room; all the detectives knew that everyone in the town and indeed the press was calling the killer 'Copycat Jack' and the 'Brighton Ripper'. And they all knew of the historic Whitechapel link.

"Yes, yes," Carter said. "Go on, Dave, please."

"Yes, skipper. Kowalski fell wayward in his studies and was moved to our own Royal Sussex County Hospital to save his career. Excellent record since arriving there; he has done well. He is openly homosexual and is well-liked by work colleagues. No previous convictions."

"Oh great," Carter interjected, "clean as a whistle thus far."

"No wait, skipper. The one thing that stood out to

me in all the statements taken by the detectives from customers in the bars is that there is a man that most call 'Jacob', whispered as known for being a source of recreational drugs."

Martin now interrupted the detective constable. "Did anyone use the name Kowalski as the dealer?"

"No, sir," Dave Smith replied. "But most of those who mentioned this dealer when questioned described this man Jacob with a profile of height, hair colour and physical appearance matching our suspect Doctor Kowalski.

And another important thing," the detective constable continued. "All the detectives who went to the pubs and clubs have mentioned in their statements that Kowalski is reported, by those who know him, to never be short of money. In addition, everyone at the hospital who knows Kowalski well has said he has lots of friends outside work and he frequents lots of the city bars. Unsurprisingly, nearly all of the persons that we interviewed said they were very concerned by the killings etc, etc. Some had heard rumours and little whispers about the case but nothing that was not hearsay. A few of them mentioned the 'Jack the Ripper' connection and a concern that there would be more murders. So to sum up, we have a drug dealer selling recreational drugs in the bars and clubs allegedly called Jacob and whose physical appearance matches our chief suspect in the case."

"Okay, Dave, well done. So, everyone, that's where we are to date. Nothing exactly concrete but with Kowalski now implicated further we must keep plugging away. Right, D.C.s Thompson, Fuller and Thomas, given what Dave has said I want you three to concentrate all your efforts on Kowalski once again. I want him checked and double-checked. My gut instinct and Sergeant Carter's is that Kowalski is our man. I'd like more of you interested in him but we are just too swamped and I can't afford to put all my eggs in one basket and miss something else. I have not given up hope that we might find a link to him from elsewhere. You are all working hard, so thank you, you know what you are supposed to be doing so get on it," Martin said. "Debrief here tonight at eighteen hundred hours, barring disasters. Fill your boots, people!"

A general ripple of chatter went around the room. Martin's phone started to ring at that precise moment. "Get that phone will you please, John? Dave Smith wants another word with me."

"Excuse me, sir," Carter interrupted his senior officer as he chatted to the detective constable a few minutes later. "It is Marshall, sir. It's urgent. She wants to speak to you; here is your phone."

"Yes, Martin. Oh, Marshall, that's great, bloody great, thank you, thank you." Everyone still in the incident room was shocked at the smile on Martin's usually thought- provoking face.

"What is it, governor?" Carter asked.

"Right, people, listen up, before you go this is important," Martin said, "perhaps a small breakthrough. Marshall has gone over the latest victim's clothing again, just to double check them and hidden in the little coin pocket on the inside of the main pocket of the victim's jeans she has found a small piece of paper. On it and written in black pen is the name 'Jacob' and a number, the number '4'. She has compared it to the handwriting on the notes left by our killer in her records and the handwriting is different. She believes this note was written by the victim himself and this would suggest he wrote it perhaps to remind himself of a meeting with a man called Jacob perhaps at four p.m."

"It fits, governor," Carter said excitedly.

"Yes, and that's what I'm hoping, John. Also," Martin went on. "The blood under our latest victim's fingernails is from a Mr. John Roberts. Marshall has sent his address in a report that will be in the file on my computer. He will need to be visited to eliminate him as a suspect as soon as possible. But Marshall did some follow-up with the hospital and Roberts was a patient there a few weeks ago. And who took his routine blood sample? Yes, our man, Doctor Kowalski!" A muttering went around the room. "Right, Becky," Martin said. "You get Mr. Roberts' details from Marshall's report and visit him; let's get him eliminated as a suspect if we can now. The rest of you keep digging for the possibility of Kowalski's drug dealing in the pubs and clubs and get as many statements as you can. If anyone names Kowalski I need to be told as soon as possible." Martin turned to his sergeant. "We, John, are going to pick up that note from Marshall," he said. "And then we are going to go and 'nick' Kowalski and this time he gets the full works, Miss Jones or no Miss Jones," he added. "I'm going to ring Flowers and tell him to postpone the press conference for a bit longer. I know the evidence is circumstantial, John, but there are just too many coincidences linking to Kowalski. Flowers told me to go with my gut."

"Well, for what it's worth, he is my gut too, governor," Carter responded.

"Thanks, John, well, if the worst comes to the worst, we will at least be knocking on doors together for the rest of our careers," he said with a cynical grin. The policeman's friend in times of such stress was always black humour, even if they directed it at themselves.

The two detectives arrived at the Royal Sussex County Hospital. Before leaving the John Street police station they had established that Kowalski was indeed working there and he would be there all day working in a pre-operation assessment clinic. Martin knew he was taking a chance to arrest Kowalski again so soon, but he had become convinced that he was the killer they sought and was desperate to prevent any other awful murders from taking place. He had new evidence in the note with the name 'Jacob' on it and was aware Kowalski had also taken the blood, as hospital samples, found under all the victims' fingernails. He had got a pretty much exact description of Kowalski from the young male receptionist at the town hall and knew a man called Jacob who also fitted Kowalski's description was dealing drugs in some of the gay bars. Kowalski was a student doctor and, as such, knew about human anatomy. To a lesser extent, he knew Kowalski had studied and was well-schooled in English. Indeed, at this time, Martin was confident he had the right man and he was going to give Kowalski a hard interview, in the hope the young man would crack and confess.

The officers' walked briskly down the hospital corridor. When they left the corridor and went into the pre-assessment ward they saw Kowalski on the far side of the large room. He recognised the two police detectives immediately and his face drained completely of colour. Martin said, "Can we have a word with you in the corridor, Mr Kowalski?"

"What about now?" Kowalski asked his voice trembling.

"I think we should have a talk in the corridor," Sergeant Carter said, taking hold of the young man's right arm firmly.

Kowalski was almost led away, as a young nurse went up to the three men. "Are you okay, Jakub?" she said.

"We are police officers," Martin said producing his warrant card. "Doctor Kowalski is helping us with our enquiries, miss," he added.

"But, he is our doctor taking blood samples," the young nurse said, now quite fraught.

"Not today he isn't," Martin replied, and they led Kowalski out of the room. As soon as they were in the corridor Martin said, "Jakub Michael Kowalski, I am arresting you on suspicion of murder," and cautioned him.

The young man had tears in his eyes. "You are wrong," he pleaded. "You are so wrong."

Without saying another word Sergeant Carter put a pair of handcuffs on the distraught young man. The pair of detectives then ushered him toward the main hospital entrance and exit. As they were walking Kowalski suddenly saw the tall figure of a man striding towards them in a white coat. He immediately recognised the figure as the stranger he had met in the bar and sold the drugs and phials of blood to. The man quickened his step seeing Kowalski was in handcuffs and obviously with the police. He turned off down another corridor just ahead of them. "It's him," Kowalski said. "He is here, he is here." Kowalski started to struggle violently.

"Stop that and calm down," Martin said. "You are already in enough trouble."

"But you don't understand. It's him," Kowalski

said, "he's here."

"Who do you mean? Who is here?" Carter said in exasperation.

"Him," Kowalski said his voice quietened.

Kowalski was in a total state of shock; not only had he been arrested for the murders he knew he had not committed, but now he was convinced he had seen the dark-haired stranger he had sold the drugs and the blood phials to and had virtually walked past this man as he was taken into custody by the two police detectives in the hospital corridor. He felt that his head was about to explode.

As he was taken into the back door of the police station leading into the custody suite Kowalski struggled again with his captors. "I'm innocent," he pleaded. "I'm innocent." Martin ignored these constant pleas from his prisoner and the three men stood before the reception desk of the gaol block where Martin proceeded to give the details for the arrest to the heavily set custody sergeant, who took down the information provided by the senior detective on the large pro-forma custody record sheet. Kowalski had now stopped struggling and knew he was in big trouble by this time. "I want a solicitor," he said. "I want a solicitor," he said again, his voice was raised and chaotic.

"Settle down, lad, you're in my cell block now," the custody sergeant said in a booming, harsh, northern tone. He then looked at Martin and Carter. "Who is his solicitor?" he asked.

"Sally Jones," Martin said.

"Lucky for you two, sir," the custody sergeant grinned. "We will get her here for you, son," he said to Kowalski. "You can go gents. He'll be alright here with me and our friendly jailer. Won't you, son?" His voice still booming and now punctuated with more than just a hint of a sarcastic tone. "Put him in cell number two, Bob, it's just been cleaned," the sergeant added, now speaking to the constable who was the duty jailer and who had just come into the room. "And we will need his clothing and get him a forensic suit to wear," the sergeant said. With that, the jailer, his large bunch of cell keys jangling, led Kowalski away out of the room and down the long corridor to the cell block itself.

Martin and Carter had only been upstairs long enough to grab a coffee and get some paperwork started on the arrest when they were told Sally Jones the solicitor had arrived at the station. "We will give her half an hour and then see if Kowalski is ready for an interview," Martin said.

"Can we crack him, governor, do you think? He is going to plead his innocence all the way I think," Carter said.

"He knows something else too," Martin added. "There is something else to this case. I hope I'm not missing it." Martin's voice was a little troubled.

"No, Kowalski is our man, it all fits, it all fits," Carter said. "You've got to believe that, sir or Jones will have him walk out of here again," he added.

"Yes, I know, John, you are right. I'm just tired, I just want this bastard so badly," he said "I'm starting to doubt myself. We know it's him, you are right it all fits."

Sally Jones and Kowalski were already in the tape-recorded interview suite when the two detectives came in. Kowalski had been talking to his solicitor and she had advised him of any suspected line of questioning and refreshed herself with her client's standing within any allegations that could be made against him. Jones knew that Martin must have got some new evidence to have arrested her client again so soon. In addition, she noticed this time, since being arrested, Kowalski was wearing a forensic suit and his clothes had been taken from him for forensic analysis, which was routine procedure for suspects in murder cases. The two detectives started the tape machine and identified themselves, the solicitor and Kowalski to the tape. They reminded the young man he was under caution and then started to question him.

"Okay, Mr Kowalski," Martin said. "Do you understand why you have been brought here?"

"No," Kowalski said.

"Well," Martin went on. "There have been three horrific murders that have taken place in the city on the following dates, those being Wednesday the fifteenth of November, Saturday the eighteenth of November and Wednesday the twenty-second of November. All the murders have occurred between fourteen hundred hours and seventeen hundred hours or between two pm and five pm if you prefer, and all these awful murders have involved the use of a specialised drug Dizampathene and we believe have been undertaken by someone with medical knowledge."

"I have not done anything," Kowalski interrupted. "Why are you telling me these things?"

"Please do not interrupt me, Mr Kowalski." Martin's tone was very short. "Let me ask the questions and then you can answer them," he added.

"Right," Martin said to the terrified young man. "Let's start with the missing drugs. I have a list here of several drugs including Dizampathene that have been taken by someone from the controlled drug cabinet in the hospital where you work. Are you familiar with these drugs, Mr Kowalski?"

"Well, of course I am," Kowalski replied. "I'm a student doctor."

"These drugs are all on a list provided by the hospital's senior pharmacist," Martin said. "And I believe you were the person who took them unlawfully; what do you say about this?" Martin's questioning was blunt and to the point. He intended to give Kowalski a hard interview in the remote hope of getting the young man to crack and confess.

"No, no, I did not, why do you keep asking me the same things over and over?" Kowalski pleaded.

"Have you any explanation for the drugs being missing then, Doctor Kowalski?" Martin continued to push the point.

"No, none at all," Kowalski said.

"Have you, throughout the last two months, had reason to withdraw Dizampathene from the controlled drug cabinet, Doctor Kowalski?"

"No, I don't know, I don't think so."

"It's a specialised drug, doctor; surely you would recall its use?"

"You are making me unsure and confusing me. No, I have not. I don't think so, I use so many drugs. I don't know."

"Okay. Do you use drugs recreationally, doctor?" Martin probed the young man.

"No," Kowalski replied.

"Do you sell drugs for recreational use then?" Martin added.

"No, no, I would not do that!" Kowalski pleaded.

"Well, we have several witness statements that give

an accurate physical description of you, Doctor Kowalski. Some of these statements, as well as matching your description exactly, repeatedly state that a man called Jacob is openly selling drugs, such as those that appear on the list of drugs missing from the hospital infirmary, in several of the bars in town. What do you say about that?"

Kowalski reacted immediately. "It's not me, they are wrong." His voice trembled, he knew he was lying but his whole life and future were on the line and he could not go back, he had to keep to his story.

Sally Jones, the young man's solicitor interrupted and said, "There are lots of young men who look like my client and live in this town, detective chief inspector, and plenty of them will be called Jacob." Her voice was curt and harsh however, she knew it was now a possibility that her client was not telling the truth. Martin was sowing doubt even in her mind. But she still had a job to do and intended to defend the young man in the best way she could.

"Alright," Martin said. "Let's move on, but before we do, Doctor Kowalski, please could you state again for the benefit of the tape that you deny you have ever taken, or had possession of for selling, any of the drugs that we have made you aware of today."

"No, I have not. I have not," Kowalski said.

"Okay," Martin now tried a different approach. "Because you are under arrest on suspicion of an extremely serious offence" – Martin chose his words to pressurise the young man – "We are currently searching your student accommodation again, this time with the aid of a specialist drug-detecting sniffer dog. Now, given these facts, are you sure you want to pursue your statement that you have not stolen, sold, or have any of the drugs previously outlined to you?"

"I never took any drugs," Kowalski said desperately. Cleverly the young student doctor had never taken any of the drugs he had stolen from the hospital pharmacy back to his accommodation, so this revelation about the drug dog being used in the search had not panicked him into any sort of a confession and, although fraught, he stuck to his story.

"Is there anything else at your student accommodation we are likely to find, doctor? Anything you want to tell us about before this matter becomes any more serious?" the senior officer went on.

"No nothing. You will find nothing, I haven't done anything," Kowalski maintained.

"So, no surgical instruments or blood-stained clothing, no string, no personalised handkerchiefs and no square white cloths… come on, doctor, now is the time to, be honest, we only want the truth from you." Martin was bombarding the young man.

"No, no, nothing I don't have those things. Why are you asking me all this? I don't have these things." Kowalski was getting more desperate.

Martin pushed home his advantage. "All our victims have been homosexual prostitutes. Have you ever visited or used the services of a prostitute, Doctor Kowalski?"

"No never. I never have," Kowalski said.

"But you are a practising homosexual are you not?" Sergeant Carter added.

"My client's sexuality is his business, detective," Sally Jones said raising her voice.

"Not when our killer is killing homosexual prostitutes and we believe your client is responsible for these murders," Martin retorted. "Answer the question, Kowalski." Martin directed his stare directly at the befuddled young man.

"Yes, I am homosexual, but I'm not a killer and I don't use prostitutes," Kowalski pleaded.

"I still object to this line of questioning," Sally Jones repeated. "The sexuality of my client is not under investigation here," she said.

Martin was now in full flow. "Do you know, or have you ever met a Marcus Robertson, Doctor Kowalski?"

"No," Kowalski stated.

"You seem very certain, Mr Kowalski," Martin added.

"No, I don't know anyone by that name. Why should I?"

"Oh, so he is not a patient then?" Martin snapped.

"I don't know," Kowalski said. "I cannot remember all my patient's names."

"What about the names of the men you kill and rip apart then? Mr Robertson was our latest victim and on his body, this note was found with the name Jacob and the number four written on it." Martin showed Kowalski the note which was sealed in a marked evidence bag but could still be read. "That is your name isn't it, Mr Kowalski?"

"Yes, yes, my name is Jacob, but it's not spelt that way."

"Oh, come on, doctor," Martin went on. "Well perhaps your friend didn't know how to spell it in Polish," he added sarcastically.

"He's not my friend. I don't know this person, why would I?"

"And the number four on the note. We have already established Mr. Robertson was killed at or near four p.m. on the afternoon of Wednesday the twenty-second of November, a date and time for which you have no alibi, Doctor Kowalski. No, that is, because I put it to you, that you were meeting Mr. Robertson and murdering him at this time and that he wrote your name and the number four when you made the appointment to meet him."

"No, no, I wasn't, I don't know this person, it's the truth the truth," Kowalski was breaking down.

"You were removing his organs one by one, weren't you, Doctor Kowalski? Look at these pictures." Martin thrust the horrific pictures in front of Kowalski again. His tactics were shocking but justified in his mind. If Kowalski was capable of such barbarism, then lying to cover his tracks would not be beyond him, and he was hoping the shock tactics would draw a confession out of desperation.

"You even removed a man's genitals, a man who had your name and the number four in his pocket and later you delivered them to a local councillor, didn't you, Doctor Kowalski, didn't you!"

"No, no, I didn't do this, I couldn't." Kowalski was nearing breaking point.

The interview had lasted for a long time and Kowalski's solicitor was now clearly seeing his distress, but in noting his perseverance in the denial of all the allegations she interjected. "So we have established there is a note with the name Jacob on it and a number four, and, as I stated earlier in this interview, there are lots of young men called Jacob in this city, detective, and the numeral could mean anything. My client has repeatedly stated his lack of knowledge of any of these events and I will be forced to advise him not to answer any further questions on this point, it has been exhausted," she added.

"Okay, so let's move on again then," Martin said. He did not want any breaks in the questioning; he had to be relentless to succeed and he intended to browbeat his suspect with further interrogation. He went on. "Once again, I put it to you, Doctor Kowalski, that I have a list of dates here, namely as I have previously stated, the fifteenth of November, the eighteenth of November and the twenty-second of November and I need to know where you were precisely on all of these dates between two and five p.m., and if you have witnesses that will verify your whereabouts at these times."

Sergeant Carter tried another psychological approach and in a soft almost gentle voice said, "This is your chance to confess, doctor, and then we can get you a coffee. You will feel better if you just tell us the truth, that's all we want the truth?"

The pair of detectives paused to allow this question to sink into the young man's mind. Then, with Kowalski's lack of response, Martin took over again.

"Up until this point you have been unable to give us a verifiable account of your movements and where you were at any of these times, doctor. This is important."

"I don't know, I don't know," Kowalski repeated, his desperation growing.

The detective proceeded to reel off, once again, labouring the point, the list of dates and times all of which correlated to the dates and times of the murders. His action was quite deliberate, and he was repeatedly throwing large amounts of information at Kowalski in the hope the young man would crack and confess.

"I've told you, I keep telling you, I don't know, I don't know, I'm telling you the truth, I am. I am."

Kowalski was at the point of crying, desperate to be believed.

"No, I will tell you, young man, why you cannot tell us your whereabouts on these afternoons and at these times," Martin said again. "It is because you were either committing these horrendous murders or delivering body parts from those catastrophic killings to a prominent local city councillor, weren't you, doctor?"

Kowalski now sat in silence, with his head in his hands.

"Are you familiar with where the town hall is in the city, Doctor Kowalski?"

"No," Kowalski replied.

"Well, you should be. We have a description that fits your appearance given by one or more persons who saw you there on the morning of Tuesday the twenty-eighth of November. Someone who saw you hand a parcel into the reception," he added. Martin deliberately avoided implicating the front counter clerk as his witness. He knew if Kowalski was a killer and he, God forbid, was released, he would possibly hunt him down to silence him at a later time. Martin also knew that Kowalski would work out the receptionist was the most likely witness, so he was playing with fire a little by revealing he had a witness, but without C.C.T.V. footage he knew he had little or no alternative.

"So, exactly where were you on that Tuesday morning? That is, to refresh your memory, the twenty-eighth of November, think carefully, doctor," Martin was getting more and more fraught with Kowalski's stalling and his indecisive replies as he viewed it.

"I was studying, I think, or on my own at my student

accommodation. I don't go out often, I like my own company. I don't know, I don't know," the young man said.

Kowalski was starting to get tearful and fraught, so his solicitor intervened to give him a break and time to recover a little composure.

"I object to your use of the insinuation that any person unknown claim to have seen my client at the town hall on the date and time you specified. Your witness, or witnesses, might have seen someone of similar physical appearance as my client but unless you have definitive proof it was my client, which you do not, I suggest you change the tactic of your questioning, detective. In addition," the frosty solicitor went on, "I suppose you have checked my client was not working on these dates and at these times," Sally Jones said abruptly. She knew exactly what the detective was trying to achieve by throwing so much information at her young client all at once.

"Yes," Martin said. "Of course we have, your client was not at work at any of these times, or on any of these days and he needs to tell us just where he was. So, I repeat, again, Doctor Kowalski, where were you on these afternoons?"

The senior detective paused for a moment, but Kowalski gave no response. "So, are you, or are you, not our killer, Doctor Kowalski? I'm asking you a straight question and I expect a straight answer?"

"No, no, I am not a killer. I have not killed anyone, I never could," Kowalski said again in a desperate fashion.

Sergeant Carter then picked up the questioning. "Right then, Mr. Kowalski, let us pick up on the facts you have told us to date. You have stated that you don't go out much. Your friends have all stated to us that you regularly go out to the bars with them, and you are well- liked and a creature of social habits. Why would they tell us this if it is not true? You are lying to us, young man, it's time for honesty," the sergeant said.

"I am being honest," Kowalski pleaded. "I have not killed anyone and I don't know anything about any drugs. I just want to go home." His voice was breaking with emotion.

The police sergeant continued. "You are a doctor and we are saying to you, that every one of these murder victims was killed on a date and time that you were not working. As well as in a manner and with instruments that you, as a doctor, would have access to.

I want you to have a look again at these photographs," Carter said. "These were once healthy, happy young men!"

He laid out the photographs, one by one of all the victim's mangled torsos for Kowalski to see.

"Look at these pictures," he said. "This is your handy work isn't it, isn't it!?"

"No, no," Kowalski cried.

He was despairing and more anguished by the shock of the sickening photographs.

"No, no, I could not do that, I'm a doctor, not a murderer, you are wrong, you are so wrong."

He was nearing breaking point and the photographs had created their desired effect. They were shocking for everyone to look at, including the young solicitor, Miss Jones.

Martin sighed, his exasperation showing and he said, "Right, so we have established that you have admitted to having no alibi for the times of these killings, and all of these poor, innocent young men have blood under their fingernails which was taken, by you, at the hospital in which you work. How do you explain that?"

"I don't know, I don't know, I can't tell you, I don't know." Kowalski was a broken man. He was for the most part being truthful, but the relentless questioning was seemingly endless. His solicitor could see that the different blood found under each of the victim's fingernails was the most damming piece of evidence the detective inspector had against her client.

"I need to talk to my client for a moment," she said. "We need five minutes alone." This was a clever and also a desperate move on her part. Firstly, she did this to break the detective chief inspectors' momentum and secondly, she wanted to see for herself if her client had any feasible explanation for this damning evidence against him.

Martin suspended the interview, recording the time of the suspension on the tape machine before stopping the tapes. "I need to get some air," he said to his sergeant.

"Yes, sir, so do I," Carter agreed.

"We will give you thirty minutes," the detective inspector said to Miss Jones, and the pair left the room.

As they went out of the custody suite, D.C. Hopkins was just coming along the corridor. He had just returned with several of the other detective constables, who had been searching Kowalski's accommodation for the second time.

"Tell me some good news for fuck's sake, Tony," Martin said, in a desperate tone to the detective.

"Nothing, governor, we found nothing. It was as clean as a whistle; no drugs, knives or anything associated with the murders. If he is our man, he has never taken anything there," he added. "We turned the place upside down, like you said we looked everywhere, every bloody inch."

"Oh, fucking hell," Martin said. "What about the drug dog then?"

"No, governor, the handler put the dog through his paces and he said, in such a small area, the dog would have easily found even the smallest trace of any illicit substance," he said.

"Perhaps he is going somewhere else," Sergeant Carter said.

"He is no fool, no fool," Martin added. "He is playing us. There is something else to this case, though. I just cannot put my finger on it. Well, anyway, John, for everyone's sake, we need this killer off our streets and Kowalski fits every profile. We just need something, just something solid. We have got to get a break in this interview at some time. If Kowalski is being untruthful, both you and I know, old friend, he will trip himself up."

"Can we risk an identity parade with the young receptionist?" Carter asked.

"I know we are desperate," Martin said. "But I checked with Dave Thompson after he took the lad's statement. He kept backtracking saying he wouldn't want to pick out the wrong man. If we risk that and he bottles it, then it is game over. How would we feel if we let the man we think is a maniac killer go unpunished and he left here a free man to kill in our community again? No, John, we need to keep pushing Kowalski, he's got to break, John, he's got to. I think we have him on the blood samples, even Sally Jones is now doubting him. I'm sure of it," he added.

With his solicitor having got him a thirty-minute break from the intensive questioning, Kowalski knew he had to find an answer to the different blood that had been found under each of the victim's fingernails. He had realised, since his first interview that this was a serious piece of evidence that could be used against him. Kowalski was a very clever young man, and he had got a little break in his fortune because he was aware that someone had broken into the laboratory at the hospital, just after he had taken the blood phials to sell. He also knew that nothing had appeared to have been taken after the incident, as being a duty doctor affiliated with the laboratory he had been one of the staff asked to check. In addition, the laboratory adjoined the hospital pharmacy and the whole thing had made Kowalski very anxious at the time because the last thing he wanted was a full drugs inventory check.

By chance, and as a great stroke of luck for the young doctor, the hospital manager, although having done an internal investigation and recorded some details of the incident, had not formally reported it to the police. She had meant to, but because nothing appeared to have been taken, it had been considered a minor incident and as a result of her heavy workload had been forgotten. Kowalski obviously did not know this fact but had remembered the incident taking place and now thought he could use this one-time break-in as a desperate line of defence to deflect the blame from himself. Now was the time he decided, to share this important piece of information with his solicitor.

Sally Jones was talking to her young client firmly. "It is important you are clear on the matter of these bloods, Jakub," she told the young man. "I need you to be upfront with me."

Kowalski proceeded to tell his solicitor about the break-in. She told her client he must bring the details of this, his latest revelation, to the attention of the detectives questioning him. She knew this new information would throw some major doubt on their prime and most significant piece of evidence against her client in this case. She, though, couldn't help wondering why the young man had not chosen to reveal this fact before.

Thirty minutes had passed and the two detectives came back into the room. Martin resumed the interview and, after once again outlining the time of the resumption and those present in the interview room, he reminded Kowalski that he was still under caution.

"Okay, tell them, Jakub," the solicitor said to her young client. "Tell them what you just told me. Go on," she said. "It is very important."

"There was a break-in at the hospital laboratory a little while ago," Kowalski said. "They said nothing was taken. But I think it was reported to the police, perhaps some drugs and the blood samples could have been stolen then and it was overlooked. I think later someone noticed some were missing," he added, putting an untruthful spin on the tale.

Martin and John Carter were stunned. It was a disaster to hear that news, even though it was very unlikely that any would-be thief would steal blood samples, it was not impossible, and it massively weakened their best possible lever against Kowalski. This, coupled with any lack of evidence found during the search of Kowalski's home address, had seriously weakened the fabric of the accusations the detectives were making towards him.

"Why have you not mentioned this before?" Martin's voice was abrupt and quite frustrated.

"Well, you are the police, I thought you must have known," Kowalski replied. He was feeling a little calmer, happy in himself that he had at least, slightly perhaps, dented the case against him.

"We will check," said Martin. "But even in this event who would break in and steal blood samples!?" the chief inspector added. "It is not the most usual of things to take."

"Someone intending to commit murders and shed suspicion from them," retorted the young man's defence council. She was now in full-on defence mode. "I think that line of questioning has run its course, detective," she added, her voice calm but emphatic. "You need to check these facts and see if any break-in works in with the timeline of these murders, don't you?" she added.

"Okay then, Doctor Kowalski," Martin said, he was now desperate for Kowalski to trip himself up. "Where do you stay when you are not working?" he asked the young man.

"At my hospital accommodation; it's where I live," Kowalski said.

The senior detective raised his voice. "No, I mean what other addresses do you stay at, perhaps when you are not working or maybe even when you are? We now have reason to believe you are using another address, maybe a friend's even. Where do you stay when you are not at home, Doctor Kowalski?" The senior detective was trying to pressure the young man by implying they already knew that he used another address.

"I only stay at my hospital accommodation," Kowalski said. "I have nowhere else to stay; why would you not believe this?" he added.

Martin and his Sergeant knew they were losing the battle of breaking Kowalski down but they were not finished with the young man just yet. "So," Martin went on. "You are a very clever young man, aren't you, Mr Kowalski?" Martin said.

Kowalski said nothing.

"Well, you won a scholarship, didn't you?" the senior detective continued. "And you are interested in English both Language and Literature," he added. "Are you a poet?"

"Oh, chief inspector!" Sally Jones's frustration was evident as she interrupted the senior officer. "This is going too far. We established my client's gift for English in our first interview, it is taking things way too far," she said again.

"Poems with historical reference were found at all our murders," the detective chief inspector retorted. "I want to establish whether your client is, or is not, responsible for them," he added. Martin himself was becoming more and more fraught; he knew he was losing this battle with both the student doctor and his solicitor, and he was starting to clutch at straws.

"So," Miss Jones went on, her voice now curt. She was sensing Martin's weakening position and was now becoming more dominant and indeed now felt she had the opportunity to be the one running the interview. Her voice now raised she said, "This interview has been going on for hours and we are back to square one; you seem to have nothing concrete to back up your allegations against my client. There are lots of men called Jacob in the city and lots more who match your description," she added tartly. "Your reference to my client's interest in English and your poetry is tenuous at best," she said. "And you have no D.N.A. evidence, as far as I am aware, against my client to date. We have established there was a break-in at the hospital laboratory, which you should have already been aware of, and a person or persons unknown could have stolen some drugs and indeed the blood samples you so deliberately used in your accusations against my client. You have a note with a name and number of little worth. No, I put it to you, detective chief inspector, that you need to find some evidence that will substantiate your accusations of his guilt, or release him again," she added confidently.

"Well, we do have some partial fingerprint evidence at all the crime scenes," Sergeant Carter said hoping this would get a reaction from Kowalski and his now confident defence council, with such a revelation of significance.

"Oh have you. Could you repeat that please, sergeant?" Sally Jones's voice was raised slightly again, indicating her obvious eagerness for the response.

Carter swallowed and thought to himself. *What is she up to now?*

"Can you confirm you have the partial fingerprints of a suspect at all the murder scenes?" she added, once again the keenness for the police officer's reply was more than apparent.

"Well, yes," Martin replied. "But they are only partial prints and they are not yet identifiable to any one individual exactly at this time," he added. With this latest revelation by the detectives now clarified to her satisfaction, Miss Jones turned to her client and smiled.

"Do you know my client has no fingerprints?" she said.

"What on earth do you mean?" Martin replied in a shocked manner.

"My client had an accident with acid as a very young child. His hands were so badly burned that the skin on all his fingers was grafted from his thighs. He has no fingerprints, none at all," she added still smiling. "If, you are basing your worthless assumption of my client's guilt on just circumstantial evidence, and as I see it any lack of a foundation of proof, I suggest he be freed again. Your indicator of partial prints at the murder scenes just reinforces my client's innocence," she added. Martin's face drained. He and his sergeant had exhausted their questioning and with the clever twists and turns, Sally Jones, the very gifted and clever young solicitor, had managed to negate all of their vital evidence.

Although they had Kowalski near to breaking point at several points during the long and difficult interview, he had not folded and they knew reluctantly they would have to find more evidence, certainly before any actual charges could be brought. "Interview suspended at sixteen ten," Martin said, recording the time of its suspension with desperation in his voice.

"For now, we intend to hang on to your client, Miss Jones, and wish for him to remain in custody," Martin added now in a more pensive tone.

"Well," said the young solicitor, her voice was no longer raised but just forthright. "I suggest you ask your superintendent first," she said, her voice emphatic once again. "Let us see if he is prepared to put his name to holding papers with only circumstantial evidence," she retorted. Her excitement in a winning position over the two detectives once again was only too clear for all to see. Martin knew with the doubts over the theft of the bloods, no definitive proof of Kowalski having stolen the drugs from the hospital and a complete lack of any evidence at all against the young man following the search of his home address, the foundation of any case against Kowalski now was nearly hopeless.

CHAPTER SEVENTEEN

Jack had settled back safely once again in his Compton Street home. By chance, he had gone to the Royal Sussex County Hospital to visit Kowalski and see if he could get more drugs and blood, as he only currently had enough left to commit two more killings. This plan, however, was now on hold. Jack knew he had been very fortunate not to be caught during this daring venture. Indeed, it was only by the luck of a few minutes that he was able to see Kowalski had been arrested and afterward make good his own escape. Jack had to take care not to be apprehended himself. His very existence depended on it.

Although their prime suspect, the young scared student doctor had been released by the John Street detectives once again. Kowalski's revelation in his interview of the break-in at the hospital laboratory had been confirmed by the hospital security manager, and the date on which it had been committed, did indeed make it theoretically possible that the blood found under the victims' finger nails at the murder scenes could have been taken at this burglary. It was also possible that during this break-in, some drugs were also stolen. In addition to these facts, there was still a lack of any other substantiated, crucial hard evidence needed to definitively prove his guilt.

The young student doctor, however, by now, was quite distraught and desperate following his release, tired from hours of relentless questioning and the frustrations of no one believing his innocence. His own solicitor, although doing all in her professional powers to assist him, was even starting to wonder if he was guilty, or hiding something relating to these awful events. The gruesome killings, their barbarism and the circumstantial evidence against Kowalski seemed overwhelming. The more of the specific details of the killings that Kowalski had discovered through his hours of interrogation, only made him certain that he knew, and had traded with the real killer. He was caught in the worst all-consuming dilemma, for without his confessing to selling the drugs and the blood to the mystery man, he had no way to clear his name. He knew that even if he did confess to this, things had moved on at such a pace that the police would probably never believe him. He also knew full well that by this time, Martin and his team were convinced he was guilty and they were focused on convicting him.

The only thing protecting him from being locked up indefinitely was the process of law the police had to adhere to.

Martin, directly after Kowalski's interview, had undertaken a detailed discussion with professionals from the Crown Prosecution Service. They had all agreed there was no chance of charging Kowalski at this time because of a lack of any indisputable evidence. For the whole police team, it was a frustrating and exhausting time, to say the least.

Life was getting no easier for Kowalski either; indeed, following his latest release from questioning, things had taken a grave turn for the young man. Somehow, through a disgruntled police source, the press had been given his name as the number one suspect in the case. To make matters worse, they had got a picture of him and now he was headline news in the local and even some national newspapers. Some were virtually calling him the 'Brighton Ripper'. The sensationalism of the story sold papers and it made money.

"Finally some good news, governor," Dave Smith said as he walked into the office of Detective Chief Inspector Martin. "A lucky break, sir, I have managed to find out who bought that bloody camera we recovered from Freeborn. It was sold to a Mr. Graham March and I have an address for him in Kemp Town so that fits thus far."

"Oh, well done, Dave," his governor's face was beaming. "Right, we need to go and visit Mr. March, John, and hope he never has sold the camera on."

The two detectives hurriedly left the police station. They climbed into an unmarked C.I.D. pound car and were on their way. Both knew the Kemp Town area of the city very well and the pair easily found the address of the block of flats that Dave Smith had provided them with. "Number thirteen, governor," Sergeant Carter said.

"Well, it fucking would be, John," Martin replied. The two detectives climbed the stairs in the high-rise block and soon found the door marked number thirteen. "Let's hope he is in," Martin said as he knocked firmly on the door. An elderly gentleman answered the door, he was very short, slim and weak-framed and wore thick-rimmed glasses; both the detectives' hearts sank a little when they saw him.

"Are you Mr. March? Mr. Graham March?" Martin asked tentatively.

"Yes, whose is asking?" the old man replied curtly.

"Police," Martin said, holding up his identification. "Can we come in please, we need to talk to you urgently," the detective chief inspector replied.

"What about?" the old man said.

"Can we come in and discuss this matter inside, sir, please? It is so unethical to talk about such matters in this corridor?"

"Oh, very well," the old man sighed and opened the door fully. Martin and his sergeant went inside and the old man closed the door behind them. "Well, sit down then if you must," the old man said. "What do you want? I'm very busy at the moment."

"Yes, Mr. March," Martin replied. "It is about your camera, the XPls220 that you purchased from a local camera shop in the town."

"That was years ago," the old man said. By now he was twitching nervously and Martin could see he was nearing breaking point. "Anyway, I lost it, a few days ago," the old man added. "What about it?"

Martin soon realised that this cat-and-mouse game could continue for ages and he did not have the time or the inclination to play such games. He tried a firmer approach.

"That camera was used to photograph the body of the victim at the recent Dukes Mound murder. I'm sure you have read about the killing in the newspapers and I believe it may have been you who took those pictures. If it was you, Mr. March, you need to tell us now, or I might think you have something more serious to hide. Such a catastrophic murder has caused vigilantes to be out on our streets. Were it to be them who found out that your camera was used to take those horrific pictures, they might not be as understanding as I am trying to be about this matter." Martin was trying shock and scare tactics to get a response. "We need to know the truth and we need to know it now, Mr. March!" The detective's voice was forceful and emphatic.

Martin could see the old man's eyes well up with tears; he knew he had got to him. Now, he just hoped the old man would be honest with them.

"Yes, yes. Oh God," the old man started to break down. "I took the pictures. But I'm not a murderer. I'm not. I'm not," he added. "Don't let anyone hear about this. I'll help you. I'll tell you anything you need to know," he said, now totally distraught.

"Okay, Mr. March, well I think we should do this down at the station. I don't want to alarm you further, but I am going to caution you, you are not under arrest, but we do need to sort this matter out, it is serious."

"Okay yes," the old man replied. "But I didn't kill anyone, anyone," he pleaded. "You must believe me."

"Let's go and sort this out, Mr. March. Do you want a solicitor?"

"No. No, I don't need one, I don't need one. I only took some pictures."

The three men arrived back at the John Street police station; both the detectives were excited by this new little breakthrough in the case. Neither considered the frail old man a major suspect in the murders, but he could potentially have a vital bit of extra evidence. Both were hopeful, inadvertently, the old man could have possibly, actually seen the killer and just not realised it. They had to know everything he had seen that fateful day.

"Take Mr. March to interview room one," John Martin said to his sergeant. "I'm going to do this interview the old-fashioned way, pen and paper. I want to get every detail the old man has and be able to keep reading it," Martin said. "I'm just going to get us all a coffee and check my computer in case we have any other things we need to follow up on. I'll meet you in the interview room. Are you happy to be the scribe on this one, John?"

"Yes, of course, governor".

After ten minutes Martin went back into the interview room with three coffees. The pair of detectives by this time had decided to treat the old man with kid gloves. They were trying different tactics after having shocked him into initially confessing to taking the pictures. Both the detectives now wanted him to feel comfortable enough to trust them. After all, Martin had already outlined they were going to treat him more fairly than any vigilantes would.

The old man was soon telling the detectives the whole sequence of events leading up to him getting the actual pictures. He admitted to regularly going to the Dukes Mound area to secretly take photographs of men who were engaging in various sexual activities. Nothing shocked these two hardened police detectives and they were not in the least interested in the old man's morality, only the facts. The detectives knew the old man was now telling them the truth in its entirety, as he confirmed using the phone box to make the call to the police to report the murder, after he had rung and informed the newspaper. He also admitted that before he had rung the police, he had left his camera in the phone box and then also collected the five hundred pounds the paper had paid him for it and the story. Martin knew if the old man had called the paper at least an hour before calling the police and waiting to get the cash, then he must have found the victim very soon after he had been killed and there was every possibility he could have seen the killer.

"So, did you photograph any other men, other than

the body of the victim on that day?" Martin asked enquiringly.

"No, sir, I didn't," the old man replied. "It was, as I recall, a damp, cold day and it had become suddenly strangely quite foggy. To be honest the visibility was a little poor. I thought there must be a heavy sea mist descending, so I didn't see anyone." He paused for a moment and then continued: "No, actually I'm wrong there was one man I saw walking down the Lower Esplanade earlier in the afternoon," he added. "But that was a bit earlier and, to be honest, I had forgotten about it. I only now have remembered him because, since talking to you, I have cast my mind back and this man, well, he came out of the mist suddenly and he walked with such purpose. I thought at the time, he must be going to meet somebody or be late for an appointment such was the speed of his pacing. I walked right past him actually and as I said he seemed to appear from nowhere, out of the hazy sea fog, yes indeed, just as I was going to the pier to get a warm drink to warm myself up. I must admit he had a strange dark aura about him, but I'd not thought about it until now," he added.

Both the detectives now showed a renewed interest in what the old man was telling them. Up until this point in the interview, he had only relayed facts to them that they already knew.

"What did this man look like? Can you remember, Mr. March? This is vitally important to us." Martin's voice was now vibrating with urgency.

"Well, yes. Let me think," the old man went on. "He was tall, yes about six foot tall, and as I recall quite handsome, which struck me at the time. Oh yes, and he had I think dark wavy hair. I should say he was about thirty years old. Yes, and he had very dark eyes. Piercing, I remember them, like coal they were," the old man said.

"What was he wearing?" Sergeant Carter asked as he now quizzed the old man with added enthusiasm. He, too, was getting excited that they might just possibly have another witness, who could have seen the potential murderer the pair of detectives so desperately sought.

"Oh, I'm not sure," the old man said. "Umm, blue jeans and a long coat; yes a smart, very smart, long black coat."

"Now think very carefully," Martin said. "Especially before, you answer this next question, Mr. March. You must be clear about this point. Could you identify this man do you think? Could you recognise him again?"

"I'm not sure," the old man said. "I only got a quick glimpse of him. I only remember him by those features that stood out to me at the time and now only because you have asked me to think back. I've told you all I know, I truly have, sir," the old man added. By now he was getting tired and feeling very overwhelmed and upset. Both the detectives knew the interview had reached its conclusion, at least for now, knowing the old man was going to tell them nothing more that could help them.

"Am I going to be prosecuted for anything?" Mr. March asked the two detectives pensively.

"Well, that is not up to us, Mr. March, and you might still be. But we will try to get your circumstances looked at more favourably. You did do the right thing in telling us all you knew in the end."

Martin was still trying to keep the old man sweet.

Just in case he could remember anything further even at a later date. Both, he and Sergeant Carter also, knew the description the old man had given them, matched closely that of their prime suspect in the case, the young student Doctor Kowalski. But Martin still felt the old man was not yet confident enough to pick him out if the need arose.

Martin was considering bringing Kowalski in for an identity parade. It was something he had to consider with such a lack of other evidence available to him at this time. He now had two witnesses to call on. Both witnesses he also knew, however, were not reliable in their certainty of his suspect's appearance, and he knew if he arrested Kowalski again he would have to be certain of a positive outcome and charge him this time. He also realised he must have the old man on his side if he had any chance of getting him to agree to such a course of action. For now, he just had to release the old man and see if he and his team could piece together just a few more pieces of evidence, before risking arresting Kowalski again and involving the young receptionist and the elderly witness in what would be a make-or-break identity parade.

By this time tensions were running even higher in the city. Demonstrators had already attacked the police station at John Street in the frustration of what they saw as a lack of police progress in the case. Bricks had even been thrown at the station and several people, including two police officers, had been seriously hurt. There were also increasing groups of vigilantes roaming the Brighton City streets every evening, hunting the killer and hungry for revenge and Kowalski was now their number one target. He knew he could not go back to his student doctor's 'digs'. He was virtually a leper of society, an outcast. In addition, the police had said he must not leave the city and he had to report to John Street police station in two weeks.

With no place to go, Kowalski tried to disguise himself in the best way he could. He mixed with groups of down and outs, swapping clothes with them to help with his drastically changed appearance. His tormented mental state and a lack of eating and sleeping just added to reinforce this new self-contrived persona. After a few days or so hiding at various locations in the city, Kowalski found himself living in a bus shelter at Norfolk Square.

The companion for Kowalski's new Norfolk Square living quarters was a fifty-year-old, homeless man calling himself Micky Crouch. Micky was an alcoholic and had been a drug addict; he was quite an ironic companion for Kowalski considering the young doctor's drug- selling past. Micky was dishevelled and filthy. He also urinated himself frequently and, as well as stinking he was violent and aggressive. His nature kept others away from the shelter they shared which helped Kowalski maintain his anonymity and, at least, for this he was grateful. The young man though now was quickly running out of money; he had bought the favour of the alcoholic to date only by purchasing and plying him with cheap alcohol. To be honest, Micky could not care less who his companion was or where he had come from so long as he had a drink. If any such companion did not have alcohol however this attitude of sharing his accommodation would certainly change.

An emotionally and physically exhausted, Kowalski was also consumed by his need to track down the stranger to whom he had originally sold the drug and blood phials. He knew only if he could gift this man to the police, that he might be able to prove his innocence. It was his last hope.

Kowalski came around the side of the bus shelter at Norfolk Square having relieved himself against the back of it. He had noticed a strange hazy fog descending around the square and thought some sort of inclement weather was approaching, so he had started walking back to see if his living companion had noticed it too. As he did so, he caught sight of a man walking with a woman and disappearing into a dingy basement flat on the far side of the square. Although he only glimpsed the man briefly in the milky thickening fog, Kowalski recognised him as Jack almost immediately. His mind started to race and he began to doubt himself. Was that him, he thought? Was that his drug buyer and the man he thought he had seen in the hospital corridor? Had he seen the stranger he so desperately sought or was the strange fog distorting the appearance of the figures? Could it be him or was he just so desperate his mind had tricked him into a likeness? He was convinced the man he sought was gay and this man was walking holding the hand of a tall blonde female. Did that mean anything? He was so unsure. His mind, by this point, was running rampant. All sorts of things were going through his head. Did he risk confronting the man? What if he was wrong? Would a rashness to do this expose his fragile identity? Would the police believe him? Kowalski started to doubt his own sanity.

Kowalski ran from the square; he was so unsure what to do next, that he found himself pacing the streets off Western Road unable to decide what he should do for the best. Nearly three-quarters of an hour passed, and the young man realised if he didn't make up his mind soon then his suspect could be gone forever. Quickening his pace he hurried back towards Norfolk Square. By now his heart was thumping so hard he could barely think above its tremor. He must know. He just must know, he thought.

Once back at the square, Kowalski made his way across to the basement flat that he had earlier seen the man and the woman go into. As he approached it he saw an old man on the steps of the flat just above smoking a cigarette, and without thinking he blurted out in a panicked almost hysterical manner, "Who lives there? Who lives in that flat there?" He pointed to the basement flat. "Do you know them? Do you?" he asked.

The old man looked down at the filthy, bedraggled young man and laughed. "You can't afford that!" he said cautiously taking a step up nearer to his front door.

"What do you mean? What do you mean? What do you fucking mean?" Kowalski responded in angry desperation.

"She won't be interested in the likes of you," the old man said. "Bloody tranny prozzy," he went on, "and very expensive, so forget it."

The old man was fed up with the comings and goings from the basement flat. He often got men going to his door by mistake, and now having a filthy vagrant demanding to know who lived in that flat had pushed him to his limits. He shook his head in considered frustration, muttered something about the sudden hazy fog and being pestered by a 'nutcase', opened his door and returned to his flat slamming the door shut.

Suddenly, it dawned on the young doctor. He shivered having realised that if his instincts were correct and this was the dark stranger he sought, the transvestite prostitute was in very grave danger. In a mad panic, he rushed down the steep steps of the basement flat, almost falling in his rush to descend them. He could see that the front door to the flat was slightly ajar, so without thinking he went inside. Kowalski found that there was a small narrow corridor that led to several other rooms. He frantically pushed the door open to the first room and then went along to the second; as he pushed that door open, he was met by the most awful scene of unimaginable human carnage.

A figure, of what appeared to be a man, trussed and mutilated beyond belief lay on a bed in the middle of the room. Beside the body was a blonde wig splattered with fresh, dark red blood. The blood-drenched torso had been gutted and disembowelled and genitals were protruding from the open mouth. Both the victim's eyelids had been removed and laid onto the right cheek of the corpse. On the left cheek of the victim's face two straight vertical lines had been neatly carved into the flesh. Kowalski's instincts as a doctor took over and in a moment of madness he leaned over the body on the bed desperate to see if he could find any sign of life. He pressed on the torso as if in a vain attempt to stop the endless flow of blood from the multiple gaping wounds. His situation and the awful shock of his discovery had lessened his senses to the point where he was acting purely on adrenalin. With a sudden realisation that it was hopeless, he stood motionless. He saw a folded note protruding from just under the body. Without thinking and seeing something written on it Kowalski picked it up. He unfolded and opened it. It read:

> *"Another whore lies ripped and torn,*
> *And you, my foe are left forlorn,*
> *To prison, you take me, but know you well,*
> *I walked a free man, from your cell."*

With a note like this, a desperate Kowalski realised he was being implicated again. He dropped the note to the floor brushing his hands together, almost as if trying to cleanse them of the writing on it. He was in shock and trembling; he staggered up and into the hallway, then went through the front door and up the steps of the flat. By this point, Kowalski was drenched in the victim's blood and he now stood at the top of the steps to the property frozen with terror. The sight of him standing loitering there covered with blood and in the eerie thickening greying fog made two passing women scream, which, in turn, alerted the attention of several men passing by, who ran hurriedly across to see what was happening. The gaunt, grey figure of what appeared to be a dirty tramp met them, his hands were shaking violently and he was drenched in blood. The old man Kowalski had previously questioned, having heard the commotion, had also come out of his flat to see what was going on.

"He has killed her," he shouted. "He has fucking killed her," he shouted again. The whole city had been shaken by the awful catalogue of the continuing gruesome killings. It was all people were talking about, and it was preying on everyone's minds. The press had labelled the murderer as the 'Brighton Ripper' and the infamy of the name had stuck. Seeing a man covered in blood and hearing such screams and the accusations that were being made, caused two of the men who were now standing nearby to grab Kowalski. They were viciously punching him and repeatedly knocking him to the ground. "He's the 'Ripper'. He is the 'Brighton Ripper'," one of the women shouted hysterically.

Within seconds, what seemed like the entirety of the city was adorned by the sound of police sirens which punctuated the afternoon air. The police had been swamped by numerous emergency calls from people who had witnessed the goings on, or others who had seen three bloodied men fighting.

The first of several marked police cars alerted to the disturbance arrived at the square. Two uniformed officers jumped from the patrol car, its blue lights flickering in the greying fog. They just seemed to abandon the vehicle in their haste to get to the scene. They ran hurriedly towards Kowalski who was now struggling violently with his two civilian captors, fighting back in what was now a desperate bid for freedom. Driven by the absolute terror of his predicament, Kowalski managed to shake himself free from his attackers. He ran quickly pursued by the two young men and the two uniformed police officers. Other police cars were arriving from all directions and Kowalski fled like a panicked animal past two more uniformed officers, who repeatedly shouted at him to stop. Running blindly, Kowalski hurried through the fog that had thickened again. In his panic, he left the safety of the pavement and ran into the main Western Road. Almost instantly he was hit by a large van travelling along it. The van and several other vehicles skidded to a sudden halt. The force of the impact from the collision tossed Kowalski like a rag doll high into the air and he came down hitting the road head-first, with a traumatising blunt thud. People were now getting out of stationary vehicles to see what exactly had happened as the traffic came to a complete stop. The van driver, who had hit the young man, got out of his vehicle. He was dazed and shaking. "Is he alright, is he alright?" The man called out in a state of panic.

All most people had seen was a young scruffy man who, pursued by police in the fog, had run into the road. They were unaware of any of the preceding events and were hostile and abusive to the police officers present. The scene was rapidly descending into chaos. "That is the 'Ripper'," one of the men who had chased Kowalski shouted, as he ran up from where he had previously been grappling with the young man in Norfolk Square. "That scruffy vagrant is the 'Brighton Ripper'," he shouted again. The whole atmosphere at the scene of the accident suddenly changed; people were now visibly shocked and many started talking amongst themselves and pushing police officers forward, hoping to get a glimpse of the infamous 'Brighton Ripper'.

Police officers continued to move onlookers away and the air was punctuated by sirens once again, this time ambulances, responding to the calls on the radio by the first police officer at the incident asking for their help. The young doctor was bleeding profusely from a gaping head wound; his blood mixing with that of the blood from the victim of the flat. He was saturated in blood. The two officers who had initially chased Kowalski were trying to get a response from him. One was supporting his head while the other was kneeling just at his side. The young man's eyes were open, but he was constantly slipping in and out of consciousness.

Sergeant Carter and Detective Chief Inspector

Martin arrived at the chaotic scene only a few minutes after the accident had occurred and got out of their vehicle. The two bullied their way with an obvious urgency to the front of a group of onlookers, who were being kept back by the multiple numbers of police officers now present. A uniformed constable let the two plain-clothed detectives through the cordon and they ran over to where Kowalski lay. Martin knelt beside Kowalski and alongside the uniformed sergeant who was supporting the head and neck of the desperately injured young doctor. The sergeant looked at the senior officer and shook his head, indicating he thought the blood-soaked young man would not make it. Martin looked down into the eyes of the fatally wounded Kowalski and put his face down to him as if in some vain hope to hear a death-bed confession.

In seeing Martin's face something in Kowalski was awakened. He managed to lift his head fractionally from the officer's arms supporting it and with a last ounce of defiance he formed his lips to whisper one word. "Innocent," he said spluttering through the blood which was by now pouring from his mouth. "Innocent," he said quietly again. His body then shook violently with a spasm, his eyes rolled upward and they were lifeless.

Paramedics, who had just got to the scene, now desperately tried with the police officers to revive the young man, but they knew it was in vain. The young student doctor and the man Martin and his team thought for certain had been the 'Brighton's Ripper' was dead.

A dark figure stood unnoticed amongst the crowd that had gathered at the chaotic scene. Jack had been watching all the events as they had unfolded. In a bizarre twist of fate, because he had just committed the murder, he had been close to the flat and had seen everything. Jack knew he had just witnessed the capture and indeed the demise of the innocent man, whom the police were convinced, was the so-called now infamous 'Brighton Ripper'. He also knew, with his perfect patsy now dead, he could relax a little and as he turned and walked away back to the security of Compton Street, he gave a cold but self-satisfying merciless grin.

CHAPTER EIGHTEEN

One week later, Jack appeared again. He stepped out the door of number thirteen Compton Street. Once more he was dressed in his original Victorian gentleman's attire. He placed his top hat on his head and closed the front door of the property for the last time. In his right hand, he clutched his precious polished black Gladstone bag and with his left hand, he removed the silver key from the lock gripping it tightly and holding it in his palm. It was early evening and the first signs of the forthcoming darkness were drawing in. The air hung with a thick damp fog, which had once again descended inexplicably across the city.

Jack strode purposefully down Compton Street and turned into Dyke Road. As he did so, he saw the recognisable figure of a dishevelled old woman walking toward him. She was dressed in the same dark shawl, which she had worn when they had met for the first time, all those weeks before and her fragility was marked in her silhouette by the dimly lit street. As they met they both paused for a second, neither one making direct eye contact. Jack pressed the silver key firmly into the palm of her gnarled left hand and the two continued in silence in opposite directions.

The old woman finally reached number thirteen Compton Street. Without hesitation, she used her bony hand to push the silver key into the lock. She turned it, opened the door, and went inside. In the small lounge, a fire had been lit and it burned in the grate warming the room. She moved to the lounge window and struggling slightly, picked up the threadbare rug which lay under the window and on the floor. She continued to hang the rug up on the improvised hooks mounted on the top of the crumbling window frame, the rug's limited purpose to obscure any view into the lounge from outside. Then she moved toward the fire, took her shawl from her shoulders and placed it on the small round table next to the tatty armchair. On the back of the chair, there was a blanket which she unfolded. Adjacent to the fireplace, the pitted glass of the full-length mirror picked up her reflection in the flickering firelight which was all that lit the room. Standing in front of the mirror, she removed the large black neck scarf, which until now had hidden all her neck and which rode right up to just under her heavily lined chin. As she did so in the dim light a scar which lay across her throat became visible. It was quite a long, horrific scar, which bore signs of being stitched, but in a chaotic and disturbed manner.

The old woman continued to get undressed and removed a cardigan and her blouse exposing her chest. Another huge, ghastly scar came into view. It ran from the top of her chest down and over her abdomen. This scar also was marked by the same healed stitching pattern and it grossly disfigured her midriff. She slipped her long dark skirt and the underlying petticoat to the floor, stepping out of them. As she turned slightly, the mirror reflected the fact both her breasts had been removed. These also were heavily marked, this time with unstitched scar tissue. Although she had no breasts this was not immediately determinable as the scaring on her neck and the front of her torso were so horrifying, her lack of breasts seemed almost insignificant. Finally coming into view, as she now lifted her head, there were two grisly scars on the woman's face. They were almost invisible when she was hunched over. The scars clearly marked where her eyelids had been stitched back into place, in a very uneven and irregular fashion.

Now completely undressed barring her knickers and well-worn shoes, the old woman raised her eyes and stared at the reflection of her disfigured body in the mirror. As she stood there, she whispered to herself, "Just one of your forgotten victims from so many years ago was I, and now chosen by you, I become your travelling companion for all eternity, my Master Jack." She reached out and took hold of the blanket she had previously unfolded and wrapped it carefully around herself before unsteadily settling herself into the tatty armchair. Sitting back she gave a huge sigh as if releasing all the life from her mangled and deformed frame and she was motionless. As the light of the fire flickered, the long mirror caught the reflection of the chair again and it was empty; she was gone, back to from where she and her master had come!

Jack arrived in Ship Street. His dark distinguished figure was walking at pace and with a renewed vigour. Once again people he passed in the street gave him scant notice, too occupied by their own agendas. Jack turned off Ship Street and went into the lanes. He soon arrived back in the dark corner just off Black Lion Street and adjacent to the Cricketers public house from where he had first appeared. The thick inexplicable fog had returned and it crept along every passageway of the lanes lingering eerily. Jack walked through it and stepped into the dark shadow thrown by the tall brick wall that had hidden his first ghostly appearance. He stopped for a second, quietly and in a haunting voice he whispered, "On to pastures new for me and you, Annie. Never do I tire of visiting this earth and wreaking the havoc of death. We travel together; there is more history yet for us to write here." Jack walked forward again toward the wall and as he did so his tall figure was lost in the fog and the darkness and he, too, was gone.

The newly slaughtered, bound-up body of a young man had been laid on the bed in the bedroom of the squalid flat. He had been dead at the most for two days and had been killed at least five days after the demise of the young student doctor who the police were so certain was their murderer and the infamous 'Brighton Ripper'. A pair of shiny leather trousers hung on a bent wire coat hanger hooked to the outside of the door frame. On a messy dressing table, there was a bundled shambolic mix of much-used cosmetic make-up in varying states of emptiness. The dressing table mirror held the reflection of a disassembled stack of business cards clearly marked, male to male massage services. Beyond the reflection of the cards the mangled and blood-drowned torso of the victim in all its horror could be seen abandoned in the room. Laying next to the body and only stained at the edges in blood lay a small white pristine cloth on which the victim's nipples had been neatly placed following their removal. The body itself lay ruptured and exposed; it was naked, disembowelled and almost unrecognisable as being of any human form. There had been a cut made in a ripping motion quite deliberately from just above the pelvis finishing at the base of the sternum. This devastating wound had been purposefully opened, with most of the internal organs having been removed and these along with the intestines were laid out along the front of the mutilated corpse.

The victim's throat had been cut and the deep forceful incision ran from his right ear across his windpipe and finished at his left ear; the wound having been inflicted so violently that it gaped open. A mixture of torn skin, flesh and cartilage created a flap through which his genitals could be seen lying in his throat, these having been removed and forced into his mouth as he lay dying. Both ears had been severed and both eyelids had been cut away and placed onto the right cheek of the corpse. There was one other very disturbing but familiar mark the attacker had chosen to leave on his conquest; as if signing his name to the horrific crime, he had carved one single straight vertical line into the victim's face on his left cheek. Under the torso was a piece of paper held down by nearly half of the removed blackened liver of the corpse. This time it was not folded, it was heavily bloodstained, but the writing on it was still visible. It read:

"The bodies of Whitechapel made my name,

Now on your streets, I've walked the same,

A wronged man caught, the blame is yours,

And now I'm gone free, ripping whores."

Back at the John Street police station, the major incident suite was being slowly shut down to return it to its normal functioning C.I.D. offices. The atmosphere in the large room at the end of the corridor was quite euphoric. The ten or so detectives and their commanding officer gathered there happily closing files, removing pinned-up photos and completing final reports, convinced they had caught their man. It had been just one week since Kowalski's death, the student doctor, who for what had seemed an eternity had been their main suspect in the case. Now things were finally being wrapped up, the emotional and physical pressure on the team was visibly lifted. The atmosphere even with a strict tyrant like Martin was so relaxed. The men openly shared an alcoholic drink with their commander, unheard of whilst on duty and during his watch. After so many hours of working with little or no break and all the drama, this case had taken a heavy toll on all involved. Part of the euphoria was also generated by the fact that the team only had two more hours on duty and all were shattered and desperate for a few days off. Martin turned to his right-hand man Sergeant Carter and said, "I'm bloody well looking forward to some rest days, John."

"Yes, sir, I think we bloody well all are," the loyal sergeant replied.

A phone at the back of the room rang and was answered by a young detective who told a group of chatting colleagues who were standing next to him to hush up as he couldn't hear what was being said on the phone. "It's for you, sir," he called out to his governor.

"It's probably Councillor Morgan," Carter jibed. "Phoning to congratulate you," he added sarcastically.

"No, it's the communications room," the young detective said.

"Yes, Martin here," the Chief Inspector said. Very suddenly and with an almost glazed look Martin's smile dropped from his face, as if a light had been turned off. He became pallid, ashen and grey. As if sensing something was wrong, the whole team stopped talking. There was a total deathly silence for a minute until Martin was heard to say into the phone. "Another body, terribly mutilated, a young male prostitute, killed in the last two days. No! Oh God! No!"

EPILOGUE

Following the unsolved case, Superintendent Flowers managed to avoid any backlash from the failure of his division to apprehend the actual killer of the victims within the city of Brighton. He was later made a chief superintendent and finally retired quietly to Hampshire.

Jonathon Morgan, the police despising councillor, went on to write a bestselling book about his experiences in the case. Whilst the engineers of his limelight-grabbing publicity stunt and close colleagues, Michael Afflick and Imba Justin, carried on working with the councillor. All three men achieved, through media and press coverage, a certain celebrity status which they enjoyed for the rest of their careers.

Mary Marshall the pathologist continued in a long and distinguished career. She finished her working life as a lecturer and had many a fascinated young student quiz her about the details of the case and its complexities. She continues in her retirement to be used by some colleagues as a go-to consultant for extremely challenging or complicated murder cases as they arise and has recently received an O.B.E for her services to the medical profession.

Tim Martin the dedicated police chief inspector never got over the despair of not apprehending the infamously so-called 'Brighton Ripper'. He knew that he had in effect hounded a young innocent man, who in the end and because of his actions as the senior detective in the case had lost his life. He was haunted also by Kowalski's last words of, "innocent: innocent". Indeed, Martin gradually sank into depression and never returned to front-line police work, instead turning to drink for comfort.

Two years to the day of Kowalski's death, Martin took his own life.

'Jack', had killed again.

Sergeant John Carter was devastated at the loss of his close friend and he resigned from the police service shortly after Martin's death. He and his wife moved away to Scotland, where he now runs a pub. He has taken to writing his memoirs on the case, reliving the investigation and going over and over the evidence of both this 'Brighton Ripper' case and other similar 'Ripper' type serial murders. Murders that he has discovered have taken place at various points throughout history and in various countries around the world.

He has concluded and remains convinced to this day; that '*Jack the Brighton Ripper*' is a killer who has travelled through time, killing at will and indeed was not of this world. And perhaps more importantly he remains certain, sometime in the future, that 'Jack' will once again…..

Be back!

All the characters in this book are fictitious.

Milton Keynes UK
Ingram Content Group UK Ltd.
UKHW020048110324
439185UK00007B/104